About the Boo

We all tell ourselves stories. These are stories about who we are, how the world works and how we relate to others. For better or worse, these stories often end up being our own identities and realities. This book presents a framework that enables the development of positive and empowering stories. It shows the role of the language we use in creating the stories we tell and how those, in turn, are connected to how we direct ourselves and manage our relationships. Defining leadership as the ability to inspire and influence through changing the narrative and stories told within individuals and teams, *Shoot the Boss* can be used by leaders, educators, parents and individuals to create positive change and inculcate emotional intelligence and attributes such as self-awareness, self-management, social awareness and relationship management within themselves and people under their care. These attributes are increasingly being acknowledged as the bedrock of happiness and success in life, be it at the competitive business world, school or at home. The book provides easy to follow guides and straightforward exercises on how to develop empowering stories and emotional intelligence at individual and organisational levels. The book is based on the latest finding in neuroscience and makes reference to many success stories both individual and organisational. The techniques described in the book were successfully used by more than 5,000 students from over 150 different countries who took my *Success with Emotional Intelligence* online course.

Praise for Shoot the Boss

"Mushtak's approach to leadership, entrepreneurship and management has made a profound and positive impact on the lives of thousands of people worldwide. The first time I spoke to Mushtak, it was clear that he was a passionate educator who, for years, was inspiring and motivating the students where he lectured. However, it wasn't until he launched his first MOOC in 2013 that the rest of the world got to know him as well. Through his MOOCs on entrepreneurship, emotional intelligence and thinking like an engineer, thousands of students rewired their brains to think positively, attempted to solve grand challenges with people they never met and changed their lives by changing their vocabulary. Always looking for new and more effective ways to educate more students, Mushtak is an inspiration to educators and engineers worldwide. It was this curiosity that led him to explore MOOCs and that first brought me and Open Learning to Malaysia. So, while it's impossible to predict where you might go and what you might achieve, I'm sure Mushtak's approach will make an impact on you as well."

Adam Brimo, Founder and CEO, Open Learning

"An engineer by training and a change agent through experience, Mushtak brings his deep knowledge and frontline leadership experience to this engaging and thought provoking examination of the role of happiness in everyday life. The book will appeal to everyone who seeks to explore their own purpose in life more deeply and to those who want to enjoy lasting success and personal fulfilment. The idea of the book is very simple; we all tell stories in our heads that end up shaping who we are. Great leaders and great companies are able to make people change their stories to be more positive and inspirational. As one of Mushtak's students most ably puts it, 'At the end of the day, the technical knowledge without a true-life understanding is the mechanics without any power.' If there is one take-away from the book, it is the power each one of us has to shape our own future by simply changing the P[roblem] word to the O[pportunity] word. Enjoy your own journey to greater happiness in the company of Mushtak."

Graham Watson, Founder, Positive Leadership Limited

"*Shoot the Boss* is a book that everyone should read, regardless of who you are or what you do. Mushtak does a stellar job in summing up and converting the art of living a purposeful and successful life into science; easily replicated, scaled and shared. I absolutely love how this book brings together both new and old knowledge and concepts and made it so relevant and more importantly, easily applied. I believe any reader, just like me would appreciate the attentive guidance provided throughout the process form introduction of concepts to the practical exercises provided in the book. I strongly recommend this as a handbook that all 21st century leaders carry along to better lead successful lives, families, teams and companies."

John-Son Oei, Founder and CEO, EPIC

"A book of fascinating insights. Mushtak puts the emphasis and lens on the critical importance of our storytelling and how we can use our minds to tell stories to increase our ability to shape and control our life. This book is a great example. In itself, be it the style of the storytelling or the content, this book excels in engaging the mind in the pursuit of being personally more productive and positive in life. In helping us shape more formidable stories for ourselves and our teams.

I loved that this book inspired me to think differently and deeply. Elegantly blending emotional intelligence with neuroscience, it offers powerful and practical hints, tips, tools and techniques allied to both theories. While not all of them were new to me, I found myself continuously stopping to take notes on what I could use both myself and in my work with others. Always a sign of a great book in my book! This book is at all times accessible to the reader even as it explores deep psychological human traits."

Mary Clarke, Director, Sticky Change

About the Author

Professor Mushtak Al-Atabi is currently a Senior Deputy Provost at Heriot-Watt University Malaysia. A passionate educator, innovator and an agent of change, Mushtak always challenges the status quo to unlock value. He pioneered the use of the CDIO educational framework in Malaysia and offered one of the first Massive Open Online Courses (MOOCs) in Asia (the very first in Malaysia) in 2013. His online classes, *Entrepreneurship*, *Success with Emotional Intelligence* and *Global Entrepreneurship* attracted thousands of students from 150 different countries. He speaks at international conferences and consults for national and multinational corporations, including banks as well as manufacturing, and energy companies, in the areas of leadership, innovation, human development, performance and technology. Mushtak is the author of *Think Like an Engineer* and *Driving Performance* and the founding Editor-in-Chief of the *Journal of Engineering Science and Technology*. His research interests  include thermo-fluids, renewable energy, biomechanical engineering, engineering education and academic leadership. He has numerous research publications, awards and honours. Mushtak is a Fellow of the Institution of Mechanical Engineers (UK), a member of the Global Engineering Deans Council and an Honorary Chair at the College of Engineering and Physical Sciences, University of Birmingham (UK).

Shoot the Boss

Leading with Stories in the Age of Emotional Intelligence

by

Mushtak Al-Atabi
Author of "Think Like an Engineer" and "Driving Performance"

DREAM BIG. BE DIFFERENT. HAVE FUN

Cover and artwork by Chong Voon Lyn
Book typesetting and design by Mike Ooi
Edited by Yvonne Lim

First Printing: 2017

ISBN 978-967-13063-1-4

Published by:
Mushtak Al-Atabi
No 1 Jalan Venna P5/2,
Precinct 5, 62200 Putrajaya,
Wilayah Persekutuan Putrajaya,
Malaysia

www.thinklikeanengineer.org

Acknowledgement

It is said that it takes a village to raise a person. How true! Here, I would like to pay tribute to those who make up my village, without them this book and other works of mine would have not been possible. My gratitude goes to all those who believed in me, taught me, supported me and impacted my life and my thinking style. I wish to start with my family, my wonderful parents, my loving wife and my amazing boys, Sarmad, Furat and Ayham. I also want to thank my teachers and all the authors who wrote all the great books that I read. Gratitude is also due to all my students, from whom I have learnt a great deal, especially those who shared the amazing transformational stories featured in this book. I also wish to thank Yvonne Lim, Mike Ooi, and Chong Voon Lyn for proofreading, typesetting and designing the book.

Contents

Preface

Mushtak Al-Atabi is a pioneer in every sense, and he wants you to be one too. Part management theorist, part engineer, part self-appointed student of neuroscience, he points out, using numerous examples and proven theories, that if we want to change – to become happier, healthier, more effective, more self-aware – then we can.

It is hardly a surprise that someone whose PhD thesis linked fluid mechanics to gallstones has such a grasp of how our biological functions affect our ability to lead and manage. I was first introduced to Mushtak's refreshing way of thinking when I watched his TEDx talk on how and why we should banish the word 'problem' from our vocabulary. (I have now banished it from mine – if you want to know why you should follow suit then look at YouTube). Watching him made me wish I had been one of the 5,000 students around the world who took his MOOC, *Success with Emotional Intelligence*. If, like me, you missed that particular boat, then no worries – read this book and you will encounter much of the learning (and even some of the students) from that course.

It might sound simplistic to suggest that rewiring our brain can be done simply by changing the language that we use, but Mushtak has gathered all the evidence to show exactly that. The stories in our head, he argues, end up shaping who we are. You can create those stories yourself; he does, often. The enigmatic title of the book refers to a paintball exercise he undertook to, of all things, get his former university ready for its next round of accreditation. Staff were taken to the paintball venue and asked questions to indicate their readiness for the inspection. Every time they answered a question incorrectly, they had to shoot Mushtak, a punishment for him not having prepared them well enough. Flipped learning? No. Evidence that thinking differently produces results.

This book suggests that one sure sign of emotional intelligence is a genuine interest in developing others. That being so, Mushtak Al-Atabi must have a very high EQ indeed, because this book is a complete roadmap to self-development. What story are you going to develop and tell? Read on, and decide.

Heather McGregor,
Executive Dean, Edinburgh Business School

Introduction

In 2013, I developed and offered a Massive Open Online Course (MOOC) that was entitled *Success with Emotional Intelligence.* The course was aimed at introducing the concept of emotional intelligence to my engineering undergraduate students. Besides the engineering students in our school, the course was made available for free to anyone who wanted to enrol online. The course ended up having more than 5,000 students from over 150 different countries.

The *Success with Emotional Intelligence* course was developed and offered to engineering students to address a number of needs. Firstly, as we educate engineers to Conceive, Design, Implement and Operate products, services, processes and systems that add value to and address the needs of users and customers, emotional intelligence is considered a necessary "skill" to enable students to work collaboratively as well as to develop empathy, which is a key requirement in creating products and services that will be used by others. Secondly, employers have been continuously indicating that emotional intelligence is something that they would like to see more of in our graduates. Employers are increasingly realising that besides technical competencies, graduates need to possess the emotional resilience, self-management, empathy and ability to manage relationships. Furthermore, beyond the job market requirements, emotional intelligence is necessary for individuals to lead happy and balanced life. Against this background, and being engineers, we started looking for a simple and robust framework that can be used to introduce and teach emotional intelligence to engineering students and the emotional intelligence framework developed by Daniel Goleman met our requirements and fitted the bill well.

Goleman's framework for emotional intelligence has four domains, namely self-awareness, self-management, social awareness and relationship management. Each of these domains has a number of traits and Daniel Goleman wrote a number of bestselling books to explain and popularise the concept, including *Emotional Intelligence* and *Working with Emotional Intelligence*. When I started developing the course materials, I realised the need to translate the different traits of the emotional intelligence framework to structured learning activities that students can perform, experience and go through to develop their emotional intelligence. So I played the role of a learning architect as I went about developing and integrating various activities to be part of the students' learning journey.

The response of students from all over the world towards the course and its activities was phenomenal. Many have reported amazing results in relation to their level of self-awareness, happiness and relationships with those around them. A survey to measure how the students perceived their emotional intelligence before and after the course indicated that the 18-week course, in general, resulted in improved levels of the different traits of emotional intelligence. Even more interestingly, when a similar survey was administered to a control group of university students who did not take the course, a decrease of emotional intelligence was reported!

My involvement with emotional intelligence was supposed to be a single course, but it ended up being a lifelong passion. I started reading, researching, writing and speaking on my experience with emotional intelligence. And the more I explored it, the more it made sense. We all pursue success and happiness and the more we search for them, the more they become elusive. This is a symptom of a major breakdown in education systems around the world that is characterised by the failure to prepare the students to live happy and fulfilling lives. Very few, if at all, have academic programmes declared their educational objectives as enabling their graduates to have balanced, fulfilling and happy lives. There may be a number of reasons. One of which is that academic institutions may have no idea of what curriculum should be used to prepare graduates to lead happy fulfilling lives. They may also assume that the provision of a good technical education, which will result in getting a good job and stable income, will somehow help the students achieve their potential and live the fulfilling lives they deserve.

I am not questioning the importance of academic excellence and the importance of inculcating mastery of technical skills for doctors, engineers, accountants and other professionals. These skills are now expected as the basis of education. However, the time we live in, with its fast pace, complex connections and challenging nature, compels us to rethink and reconsider how successful we are in preparing ourselves and our youth for life.

In his 2016 New Year message to educators, the Dalai Lama stressed the importance of educating the children so that they may have a realistic opportunity to change the world.

"We all want happiness and to avoid suffering, and within ourselves that involves a greater sense of love and compassion. As far as the external world is concerned it will entail taking serious steps to preserve the environment and adapt to climate change. These days, scientists are increasingly finding evidence that cultivating love and compassion has a positive effect on our physical health and general well-being. Humanity is made up of individuals and we will only achieve a happier more peaceful society if those individuals are happier and more peaceful within themselves," the Dalai Lama said.

He goes on saying, "I am optimistic about this. I believe that human nature is fundamentally positive and again scientists are finding evidence to support this. Experiments with infants, who are too young to talk, and so have limited conceptual thinking, show that they respond favourably to illustrations of people helping each other.

They show clear adverse responses to illustrations of people harming or obstructing each other. What's more, scientists have shown that constant fear and anger has a damaging effect on our immune systems.

"We may conclude that human nature is essentially compassionate. Love and affection are essential because we all depend on others to survive. Therefore, affection is part of our basic nature. If it was otherwise and it was our nature to be angry and hateful, there would be little we could do, but because it is our nature to be affectionate and compassionate it's possible for us to think of enhancing these natural qualities through education and training."

Another mystery that is worth exploring is the disconnect between IQ and academic performance and real life success. This is symbolised by the observation that many of those with average IQs are able to outperform, in life and work, those with higher IQs. There is a solid body of research indicating that the missing link in this equation is emotional intelligence which is possessed by highly successful individuals regardless of the level of their IQ.

There seems to be a convergence of a number of undercurrents indicating that emotional intelligence is poised to be a major theme of this century. I predict that more and more schools and academic institution will start paying more attention to emotional intelligence and the development of emotional wellbeing of their students when it comes to curriculum design and delivery.

I received many requests from those who participated in the *Success with Emotional Intelligence* course to compile the experiences that we had in a book and here I am obliging. In some respect, this book is an enhanced and expanded version of the *Brainology* and *Emotional Intelligence* sections of my book *Think Like an Engineer*.

This book is aimed at introducing emotional intelligence in a practical manner, providing exercises to develop and nurture emotional intelligence in a variety of contexts including home, school and work. This book also presents a holistic framework that explains how emotional intelligence is rooted into the narrative and language used by individuals and groups. This can provide a structure for change management and transformation, both at individual and organisational levels.

The book starts by describing our current understanding of how the brain works and the role of the language we use and our internal narrative in the way we think, feel, behave and manage our relationships. After introducing the framework that integrates language, narrative and emotional intelligence, stories illustrating how the framework can be used in variety of contexts are provided. A number of stories from the students who took the *Success with Emotional Intelligence* course are featured too.

(This page is intentionally left blank)

1

Homo Relator: What Makes Us Human

"It's like everyone tells a story about themselves inside their own head. Always. All the time. That story makes you what you are. We build ourselves out of that story."

Patrick Rothfuss, *The Name of the Wind*

When I was a child, the thickest book I owned was the *Arabian Nights*. It had a white hardcover and beautiful rough yellow pages and it came in two volumes. I proudly displayed it on my bookshelf and read it over and over again. Even now, every time I think of that book, I can almost smell the distinctive smell of its papers. The book revolves around the story of King Shahryar who lost trust in all women when he found out one day that his beloved wife was unfaithful to him. After executing her, he resolved to marrying a new virgin each night and ordering her beheading the next day. This way the king would ensure that his wife would have no chance to be unfaithful. As the kingdom started to run out of virgins worthy of marrying the king, Scheherazade, who was the daughter of one of the top officials of the state offered herself to be the next bride and assured her father that she had a plan. Scheherazade was beautiful, well-spoken and highly educated. She read books in many languages and she knew stories from different and far away kingdoms. On their first night,

Scheherazade offered to tell the king a story to entertain him and the king accepted. The story was magical, fun and amazing and within the story there were other characters who told their own stories, this way Scheherazade ensured that story was able to go on. On that first night, and from then onwards, and just before dawn, Scheherazade stops the story at a selected inflection point leaving the King eager for more and longing to know what will happen next. Every time the king decides to postpone her death until she finishes her story, she remains alive for one more day. In her stories, animals spoke, magic lamps housed genies who fulfilled wishes and flying carpets soared high. The story went on for one thousand and one nights, a time during which Scheherazade had children with the King and earned his trust and ultimately, she saved her life and the lives of many other innocent girls.

While the stories in the *Arabian Nights* are but a collection of myths, it is not only King Shahryar who is captivated by a good story, good stories fascinate all of us! That is why we watch movies and find listening to gossip irresistible. Our love for stories seems to have a neurological basis and I shall devote this chapter to explore the human brain from a storytelling angle. This will be helpful as we attempt to develop a framework that will enable us to understand how narratives and stories shape who we are and how they are grounded into the way our brains are wired. I will also dedicate space to explore how we can influence the stories told at individual and organisational level to enable the achievement of success and happiness.

The Human Brain

The human brain is the most complex and remarkable object in the universe. While it weighs around 2% of the body weight, it consumes 20% of the energy used by the body. On average, it has 85 billion neurons and those neurons have the ability to connect with each other in endless ways and configurations. These limitless connection patterns and interactive possibilities among the neurons enable the electrochemical activities that give rise to all our mental capacities, emotions, thoughts, memories, consciousness and the emergence of the mind itself.

We have always understood the human brain as an important component in making us who we are and how it differentiates us from other animals. The brain is behind both intelligence and consciousness; the combination of which makes us the special species we are. Efforts to understand how the brain works and how we think stem from neurologists, psychologists, cognitive scientists and even engineers. As a matter of fact, the National Academy of Engineering (NAE) in the United States, declared "Reverse engineering the human brain" as one of the Grand Challenges for Engineers in the 21st century [1]. The last few decades represented a golden era for our understanding of how the brain works. While we are still far from unlocking all the brain's mysteries, we managed to have an unprecedented access to how the human brain works and how it is structured and organised. Scientists, of many domains, are still working hard in pursuant of the ultimate explanation of what makes us humans.

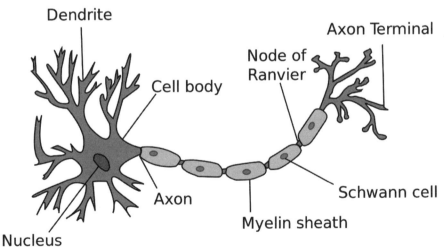

The Neuron. (Source: Wiki Commons)

Brain Functions and Structure

Neurological research has made many advances in recent decades, backed by technological wonders such as fMRI (Functional Magnetic Resonance Imaging) machines, where the brain of an individual is scanned while that individual is performing a certain mental task. Knowing which part of the brain is engaged when each mental task is performed, we can now map different areas of the brain to the variety of activities that we perform and approximately know which part of the brain is activated when we are engaged in a certain mental activity. Studying brain disorders and traumas also contributed to our understanding of how the brain works. Patients who have certain part of their brains damaged due to trauma or stroke may lose certain functions and through that we can infer that this area of the brain plays some role in the lost or affected function.

The prevailing understanding of the human brain is that it represents a very flexible system. It has a huge growth and learning potential and it continues to change throughout the lifetime of an individual, responding to different challenges and activities, continuously forming new connections between its different neurons. Neurons are responsible for transferring electro-chemical signals within the nervous system, enabling the emergence of the mind and the computing power of the brain that manifests itself as thoughts, predictions, decisions, memories, emotions and physical activities. The flexibility of the brain is an attribute of its capability of creating billions and billions of combinations of connections between brain neurons as we learn new things and have repeated experiences. It is now well established that we can "sculpt" our brains to be happy, positive and successful through intentional actions as well as mental and emotional exercises.

One way to imagine the neurons in the brain is to imagine a bunch of electrical wires. Some of these wires have insulations but a considerable number of them are not well insulated. Because of this, neurons leak electrical signals to neighbouring neurons as the signal passes through, weakening the signal. That is why when we start learning a new skill, for example riding a bicycle, it feels awkward at the beginning as the signals carried from the brain to different parts of the body get weakened along the way, but as we keep on repeating and practicing, a substance called myelin starts to form around the pathway of the electrical signal as it travels. Myelin is an electrical insulator and as more layers of myelin are wrapped around the neuronal pathway, an equivalent of a signal highway is created, where very high speed neuron firing occurs. This is the reason why we get better at doing things as we practice them, and this is also why it is difficult to change habits. In neuroscience, the saying goes "neurons that fire together, wire together."

Myelin formation starts at the 14th week of the embryonic development and continues throughout life. The growth of myelin during the embryonic stage ensures the "programming" of the basic capabilities that an infant will need upon birth. Compared to babies of other animals, human babies are born more vulnerable and with little capabilities; a baby gazelle, for example, is born able to stand, walk and run quickly while a human baby needs a year before they begin walking. This is an indication that the neuro-circuitry for walking is yet to be myelinated in humans upon birth. Although this may seem as a disadvantage at first, in actual fact the lack of myelination at birth is a powerful advantage. It gives the human brain unlimited potential as we are able to programme our brains through inducing the formation of myelin through neuron firing. This makes the human brain highly adaptable and enables individuals to master a highly-diversified number of skills and professions.

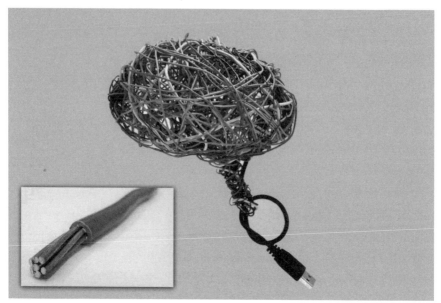

Myelin is Like the Insulation Around Electric Wires

So, whether learning how to play golf, how to play the piano, or how to drive a car, we are essentially building myelin around the pathways of the electrical signals needed to control the muscles responsible for performing these tasks. Myelination results in better, faster and more targeted neuron firing sequences, and hence mastery of the skill. Interestingly, the same process works for intentional and non-intentional actions, so if we keep on repeating a routine long enough, myelination will lead to the wiring of our habits and mental models.

As mentioned earlier, the brain is extremely complex and our journey to understand its structure and organisation, let alone its functions is still at its beginning. However, for the purpose of this book, a simplistic categorisation of the brain structure is both useful and sufficient. There are generally two ways to categorise the brain structure, bottom-up and left-right. These are outlined in the sections below.

The Brain from the Bottom Up

If we take a cross section of the brain along the body's plane of symmetry, three distinctive regions of the brain can be identified. The first brain region is the brain stem which is the bridge between the spinal cord and the brain and the gateway for all signals and sensations coming into and out of the brain. Because it is similar to the brains of reptiles, this brain region is called the reptilian or old brain. Sitting on top of the old brain, is the next brain region called the middle brain, followed by the final brain layer, the new brain. If you imagine the brain as a cone of ice-cream, the first scoop will represent the old brain; the second scoop will represent the middle brain; while the new brain will be represented by the third scoop. It is useful here to mention that mental activities are the result of very complex processes and interactions and often even the simplest decision involves multiple areas of the brain working together. Now let us examine the main features of each brain region from the bottom up.

The Old Brain

The old brain is directly connected to the spinal cord. In this part of the brain, the basic survival instincts are hardwired. The old brain is rather automatic and it gets activated in the event of perceived danger and life-threatening conditions. We have very little control over this area of the brain. The old brain is responsible for the split-second decisions we make when a car is about to hit us, or if we suspect that a venomous snake is about to attack us. The old brain is all about survival; it gets really activated when we feel danger and it quickly responds to negative stimuli. If we were to briefly describe it, we could say it is fast and selfish, because it acts quickly and only in self-interest. As it represents the gateway to the other parts of the brain, the old brain takes over our reactions in case of danger and responds automatically, this is what we call the fight or flight response.

The Middle Brain

The middle brain is the part of the brain where emotions reside and are managed, and where social cues are processed. It is responsible for processing how we feel and it is not capable of processing language (more about language processing in the next section). This may be the reason why we often find it difficult to express our feelings and emotions in words. This part of the brain plays a key role in decision making. Contrary to the common belief, humans make many of the moment-to-moment decisions based on emotional rather than rational reasons. From a computational point of view, this simplifies and quickens the process of decision-making. This has huge implications for politicians, marketers and educators who would like to influence the behaviour of others. We vote, buy and learn when we "like" what we see, hear and what we are presented with.

The New Brain

The outer most layer of the brain, the new brain, is the part of the brain that is mainly responsible for high level reasoning such as mathematics, language, perception, imagination, art, music, and planning. It is very analytical and slows the process of decision making. It is the rational brain, also called the neocortex. This layer of the brain is fully developed only in humans and it's what really sets us apart from other primates.

Emotions

Stimuli that our environments throw at us are transferred as electrical signals that travel through the nervous system and the spinal cord to the brain. Everything we touch, smell, hear and see follows this pathway. The first part of the brain that receives incoming signals is the old brain. This enables us to quickly respond to threating situations as the old brain takes over our responses. Stimuli that are not perceived to be threating progress further into the brain to the next stage, the middle brain. You can imagine that such architecture was very beneficial for our ancient ancestors who lived in danger-filled environments and needed to make fight or flight decisions on a daily basis.

Signals that don't seem to be conveying danger, will progress through the middle brain to be processed for emotions and social cues contained in them. Only after passing through the middle brain, will signals reach the new brain for processing.

Let's try to convey this with a simplistic example, suppose you were walking towards your next appointment in the city and you hear someone shouting behind you while rushing to reach out to you. Your first reaction, processed through your old brain, would be fear and anxiety. Your heartbeat accelerates and you may turn around to investigate what is going on. As the middle brain kicks in, you are trying to assess if the man is shouting in anger or excitement, using other social and emotional cues you may gather as the situation develops. If the situation is still unclear, the new brain gets engaged. Could this be the cashier from the coffee shop where you just bought your ice blended coffee from and he is giving you back your phone which you have just forgotten? Suddenly, you feel happy and grateful and you start thanking the man profusely.

This architecture of the brain has deep implications for the role of emotions in thinking and how can we rewire our brains. As signals go through the old and middle brains before reaching the new brain, emotions will always colour our thoughts and impact our decisions. And as the new brain is the only part of the brain that is capable of processing language, we can force the flow of signals to be directed to it by describing our emotions using language. So, while our old brain always asks questions of the order: is this dangerous, is this bad for me? We can always use our language to train our brains to build more positive thought patterns that reduce our stress level and help us realise the abundant opportunities available all around us.

As mentioned earlier, contrary to common belief, the emotional brain plays a key role in the decisions that we make. This was illustrated by the case of a patient known in neuroscience literature as Elliot. Elliot had a surgery to remove a small tumour from his brain. His doctors were very pleased to note that the surgery did not impact Elliot's cognitive capacities or speech. However, strange things started happening to Elliot after the operation. He started to endlessly debate each and every detail in his life. Decisions such as which shirt to wear or which way to take to work took Elliot hours to ponder. Even simple things like whether to use a black or blue pen to write became stressful decisions, and Elliot weighed all their pros and cons before settling on the colour to use. Elliot was eventually sacked from his job and his wife divorced him. Closer examination by neuroscientists revealed that although Elliot's new brain was doing a good job at the rational side of decision making, the surgery somehow disconnected Elliot from his emotional brain. Losing that "gut feeling" or "like or dislike" feeling that we all have when faced with everyday life decisions; rendered Elliot incapable of making any decision without going through detailed analysis. Drawing from Elliot's story, it is seen that in order to lead happy and successful lives, it is essential that all parts of our brain work together in harmony. It is also important to understand the limitations of our thinking so that we can improve its quality.

The above quick and brief description will prove useful as we explore areas such as emotional intelligence, communication, teamwork and human interaction later in this book. It is useful to reiterate here that the brain works like an orchestra with all its parts contributing to the thinking symphony. So, the three regions of the brain are always collaborating to respond to the continuous stream of stimuli that we call life.

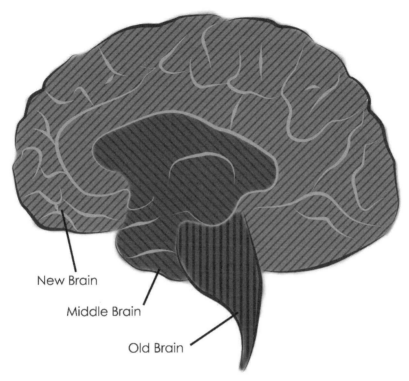

New Brain

Middle Brain

Old Brain

The Old, Middle and New Brain.

Left Brain, Right Brain, Split Brain

Beside the three layers of brain tissue that we discussed in the previous section, we know that the brain has two different hemispheres, the left (which controls the right half of the body) and the right (which controls the left half of the body). These two hemispheres are connected by a tissue bridge that is called the corpus callosum. While we feel like a single individual with a single brain, in many ways, we actually have two! Thoughts, memories, and emotions cascade throughout the entire brain, but some tasks are handled better by one side than the other.

The right hemisphere is mainly in charge of spatial abilities and image processing which includes recognising faces. It also processes music and interprets context and tone of voice. The right hemisphere thinks in images, focuses on the big picture and most interestingly, it is incapable of speech! It lives in the moment and has little concept to passing time. For the right brain, each moment is rich with emotions and sensations and that is how we have the ability to remember key moments of our life. The right brain is carefree, spontaneous and very absorbed in the present moment and what possibilities it can bring, it relishes finding connections and relationships amongst different concepts, that is why it is largely associated with imagination and creativity.

In contrast to the right hemisphere, the left hemisphere is very methodical and analytical. It thrives on details. It takes the rich moments created by the right brain and strings them into a meaningful sequence that tells a coherent story. Unlike the right hemisphere, the left hemisphere is capable of handling spoken language and it is the part of our brain that is responsible for communication and for the inner dialogue that we continuously have. The left brain compares the current moment to the past and tries to predict the future, in the process creating the concept of time. It spends most of its time analysing the past and pondering the future and it excels at logic and mathematics and retrieving factual information from memory.

It is worth mentioning here that functional differentiation between the two brain hemispheres largely holds in majority of the population, but there exists a small minority of individuals that have their brain hemispheric functions reversed.

The Harvard brain scientist Jill Taylor reported her experiences of having a stroke in her book *My Stroke of Insight*. In the morning of the stroke she had a haemorrhage in her left brain that periodically took her left brain offline giving her the opportunity to experience her being as perceived by her right brain alone. She described this in a TED talk she gave after her full recovery. "… I lost my balance, and I'm propped up against the wall. And I look down at my arm and I realise that I can no longer define the boundaries of my body. I can't define where I begin and where I end, because the atoms and the molecules of my arm blended with the atoms and molecules of the wall. And all I could detect was this energy." Jill told a fascinated audience.

"And I'm asking myself, 'What is wrong with me? What is going on?' And in that moment, my left hemisphere brain chatter went totally silent. Just like someone took a remote control and pushed the mute button. Total silence. And at first I was shocked to find myself inside of a silent mind. But then I was immediately captivated by the magnificence of the energy around me. And because I could no longer identify the boundaries of my body, I felt enormous and expansive. I felt at one with all the energy that was, and it was beautiful there.

"Then all of a sudden, my left hemisphere comes back online and it says to me, 'Hey! We've got a probelm! We've got to get some help.' And I'm going, 'Ahh! I've got a probelm!' So, it's like, 'OK, I've got a probelm.' But then I immediately drifted right back out into the consciousness and I affectionately refer to this space as 'La La Land'. But it was beautiful there. Imagine what it would be like to be totally disconnected from your brain chatter that connects you to the external world." Jill said. [2]

It is useful to reiterate here that while different hemispheres are better equipped to handle certain mental tasks, it's the collaboration and the back and forth bouncing of electric signals that results in the emergence of our mind and our personalities. Strange things happen when a person's brain hemispheres are disconnected, making the information transfer between the two hemispheres impossible. The procedure to surgically disconnect the two hemispheres of the brain is called corpus callosotomy and is sometimes performed as a last resort to treat severe epilepsy which is untreatable using drugs. This procedure was pioneered by Dr William P. van Wagenen in the 1940s and it was based on the insight provided by the observation that some patients with severe epileptic seizures show improvement when a tumour grows in their corpus callosum, an indication that dampening the storm of electrical exchange between the two brain hemispheres reduces the overall electrical activity and improves the epileptic condition.

Patients with split-brains appear normal with no observable behavioural or cognitive change. They are able to keep their jobs and engage in meaningful interactions and conversations with others. These patients also provide an interesting promise of furthering our understanding of the human brain and how it works. Psychologist Michael Gazzaniga at the University of California at Santa Monica was one of the first researchers, alongside Roger Sperry, to enlist the help of split-brain patients in his work. In his book, *Tales from Both Sides of the Brain*, Michael Gazzaniga describes a number of experiments that he pioneered to understand split-brain patients. [3]

In one experiment, patients were put in front of a screen designed to flash certain words to either the left or the right visual fields. When the word "face" is flashed to the left eye and the patients asked what they saw, they answered that they did not know. Strangely enough, if they are asked to draw what they saw using their left hands, they would doddle a face. Then, seeing the face with both eyes, they would realise that they saw a face. What happened here is that word "face" was processed by the right hemisphere of the brain, which is incapable of speech. The same hemisphere, however, controls the left hand and that is how it was able to draw what the right hemisphere saw.

In other words, the two brain hemispheres' interaction that was supposed to happen through the corpus callosum took place on the paper on which the face was doodled. It is now well documented that the sense of normalcy exhibited by split brain patients is a result of the two brains queuing each other. So, when a signal to stand up is initiated by the left brain, the right half of the body starts the sequence for standing up. Sensing the impending motion, the right brain instructs the muscles in the left half of the body to respond appropriately and so on. Therefore, the communication between the two hemispheres take place outside the brain without the brain realising that!

These experiments performed by Gazzaniga led him to a lifetime passion for studying the split-brain condition. He kept on designing more experiments through which he literally spoke to each hemisphere of the brain individually without the knowledge of the other hemisphere!

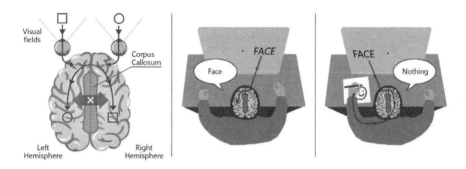

Split-Brain Experiment

In another experiment, split-brain patients were shown the words "bell" to the left visual field (right brain) and "music" to the right visual field (left brain). When the patients were asked to select an image related to what they saw from a list of four photos using their left hand, they will point to the image with a bell. They ignored other photos with even closer musical connection such as a piano, a violin, and a trumpet. This is expected as the right brain which received the visual from the left eye instructed the left hand to point at the photo with a bell as it is unaware that the word "music" was flashed to the left brain.

The amazing thing is that when the patients are asked why they chose the image of the bell, the left brain (the one capable of speech) confabulates a story that will make sense of the choice they made by saying something like "it was because the last music I heard was coming from the college's bell towers." The right brain saw a bell (through the left eye), and it told the left hand to point to it, but the left brain saw the word music and was now fabricating an explanation for disregarding the other pictures that were better related to the music theme.

The side of the brain in charge of speaking (left brain) saw the other side points out the bell, but instead of saying it didn't know why, it made up a reason! The right side was no wiser, so it went along with the fabrication. The patients were not telling lies or trying to be deceptive, they genuinely believed what they were saying. These patients deceived themselves as well as the researcher but had no idea they were doing so. They appeared congruent and never felt confused or dishonest.

In another experiment a split-brain patient was asked to perform an action only the right hemisphere could see, and the left hemisphere once again explained it away as if it knew the cause. When the words "stand up" were displayed to the left eye; the patient stood. Asked by the researcher why he got up, the subject said, "I need to get a drink." When the same patient's right brain was asked to wave, he did that and when asked why did he wave, he said, "I thought I saw a friend." In another test, a violent scene depicting someone being pushed into fire was displayed to only the right hemisphere (through the left eye). When asked to describe her emotions, the subject said she felt nervous, fearful and uneasy and attributed her feelings to the way the room was decorated.

We now know that the left side of the brain, where speech is processed for majority of the people; is also responsible for interpreting our experiences and behaviours as well as making sense of what we are doing and going through. It is responsible for narrating and directing the story of our lives and our existence, ensuring that we remain sane. It helps us make sense of the world and our role in it, how we interact in it with other people, and our surrounding circumstances.

As discussed in the previous section, emotions are processed deeper in the brain (in the middle brain, closer to where the brain connects with the spinal cord). This implies that at a deeper level, the brain tissue from both hemispheres could still communicate, even when the corpus callosum is severed. However, only the left hemisphere is able to describe the undercurrent of our existence and explain what both hemispheres are instructing the body to do.

Homo Sapiens or Homo Relator?

The scientific name that we, modestly, gave to our species is Homo Sapiens, which means "wise man" in Latin. This is based on the assumption that we are rational beings when it comes to how we lead our lives, make our decisions and choose between alternative options. Interestingly, recent scientific work started challenging this assumption, and while we are very intelligent creatures, we might be far from being the rational beings that we claim we are. Instead, what make us really stand out and enable our intelligence to flourish is our ability to collaborate with others. This collaboration is often powered by the common stories that we tell. Hence, a better name for our species might be Homo Relator or Storytelling Man. We shall explore this concept further in the following pages.

You may have noticed that you always talk to yourself in your mind. This relentless inner dialogue starts from the moment you wake up until you fall asleep. Everybody does this and it is very normal. As explained earlier, this is your left brain doing its job making sense of your existence. It is working on creating a coherent story of your life, just as it was elucidated by the split-brain patients. This inner dialogue represents the undercurrent of our thinking, how we see the world, and how we apply our logic and values to situations, people and events. Simply put, this inner or internal dialogue is the series of stories that we tell ourselves. These stories can fall into two main categories, the first one contains stories about who we are and what we are capable of; and the second one is about how the world around us works and interacts with us. These two stories are extremely important as they make up our identity and how we perceive and work with others and operate in the world. Our values are weaved into these stories and we craft them over a lifetime. Events and experiences as well as other people contribute to the storyline. In her book *My Stroke of Insight*, Jill Taylor, whose TED talk we explored earlier, described how the stroke affected her left hemisphere, and took her left brain offline, and stopped her internal dialogue. "In this altered state of being, my mind was no longer preoccupied with the billions of details that my brain routinely used to define and conduct my life in the external world. Those little voices, that brain chatter that customarily kept me abreast of myself in relation to the world outside of me, were delightfully silent. And in their absence, my memories of the past and my dreams of the future evaporated. I was alone. In the moment, I was alone with nothing but the rhythmic pulse of my beating heart." [4]

In summary, the left brain interprets our experiences and tells stories that represent an important mechanism for creating our identities and even our realities. This interpreter system weaves meaning and values we believe in into stories that ultimately drive how we manage our responses to what life throws at us, how we perceive ourselves and what are we capable (or incapable) of and how we develop our relationships with others.

These stories are told both at individual levels as well as the group levels. As a matter of fact, narratives and stories told at the community level are essential for it to function effectively. In large groups, such as nations and societies where not everyone is directly related, or at least personally knows everyone else; holding on to common narratives and stories is indispensable.

This realisation can have a profound impact on how we perceive human performance, success, achievement and happiness, both at individual and group levels. It can help parents, educators and leaders motivate those under their care and transform individuals, organisations and communities through enabling them to achieve their full potential.

In the following chapters, we will develop a framework that is aimed at understanding how stories and language drive human behaviour, performance and achievement. The framework is intended to enable humans to flourish through balancing success and achievements with happiness, meaning and positive relationships.

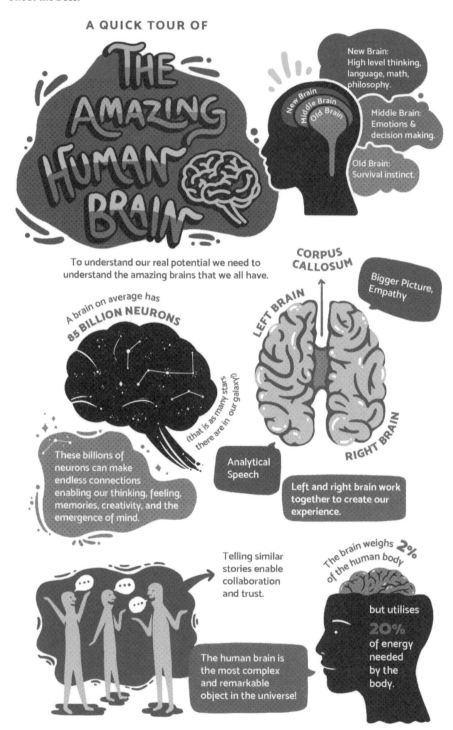

A QUICK TOUR OF

THE AMAZING HUMAN BRAIN

New Brain: High level thinking, language, math, philosophy.

Middle Brain: Emotions & decision making.

Old Brain: Survival instinct.

To understand our real potential we need to understand the amazing brains that we all have.

CORPUS CALLOSUM

Bigger Picture, Empathy

LEFT BRAIN

RIGHT BRAIN

A brain on average has 85 BILLION NEURONS

(that is as many stars there are in our galaxy!)

These billions of neurons can make endless connections enabling our thinking, feeling, memories, creativity, and the emergence of mind.

Analytical Speech

Left and right brain work together to create our experience.

Telling similar stories enable collaboration and trust.

The brain weighs 2% of the human body

but utilises 20% of energy needed by the body.

The human brain is the most complex and remarkable object in the universe!

2

What Story are You Telling?

"And I must say, there was both freedom and challenge for me in recognising that our perception of the external world, and our relationship to it, is a product of our neurological circuitry. For all those years of my life, I really had been a figment of my own imagination!"

Jill Taylor, *My Stroke of Insight*

For the first half of the twentieth century the prevailing belief within the athletic community was that it is impossible to run the mile in under 4 minutes. Not difficult, not dangerous but outright impossible! The athletic community thought that the human body couldn't physically go that fast and that it would collapse under the pressure if such an attempt is made. This was the conventional wisdom, the story that doctors, scientists and athletes told, and the whole world accepted, that is until Roger Bannister broke the record on 5 May 1956 achieving a time of 3:59.4 seconds. On that day, Bannister did not simply break the record, he literally changed the story. Suddenly, the 4 minutes was no longer a barrier and the story became "with hard work, planning and relentless execution, the 4-minute record can be broken." This had an immediately profound impact on the track and field athletes; just 46 days after Bannister broke the record, Australian John Landy beat his time! The time to run the mile kept reducing and currently, Hicham El Guerrouj is the men's record holder with a time of 3:43.13 seconds.

The fact that almost immediately after Roger Bannister breached the 4-minute barrier, other athletes did the same is a testament to how powerful the impact of the mental barriers is on what we can do and how changing the stories we tell ourselves can change our reality. Clearly, the most important impact of Roger Bannister's achievement is the mental change it created in the minds of the athletes and the athletic community at large. This ability to tell and believe stories seems to be a unique human attribute that is a function of the human brain.

We shall return to this theme of the stories told by the brain frequently in this book as we develop the framework that describes how the language we use and the stories we tell impact our performance in life. These stories affect how we manage ourselves and our relationships, for better or worse and how we can be in control of the entire dynamic.

The human outlook consists of two main constructs, namely self-management or the way we behave and deal with ourselves; as well as relationship management or how we treat others and how effectively we work with them. These two constructs are highly affected by the stories we humans tell. If you imagine our existence as an iceberg, the self-management and relationship management can represent the visible part while the stories that are told in the background of the mind are in the submerged part. It is easier to explain how this structure works with a negative example. In times of war and conflict where horrific crimes such as genocide are perpetrated, researchers observed that these crimes are always preceded by a change of how the perpetrators perceived the victims. In order for humans to inflict harm on other human beings, something that is against our nature, stories need to be told first positioning those at the receiving end of the oppression as less than humans. In his book

Less than Human, David Livingstone Smith explains that "human beings have long conceived of the universe as a hierarchy of value, with God at the top and inert matter at the bottom, and everything else in between. That model of the universe "doesn't make scientific sense," says Smith, but "nonetheless, for some reason, we continue to conceive of the universe in that fashion, and we relegate non-human creatures to a lower position on the scale." [1]

Then, within the human category, stories about hierarchy have been told enabling atrocities such as slavery, the holocaust and multiple genocides. These stories evolve gradually with catastrophic consequences. They often start by "we" are different from "them" and move on to stereotyping the "others" by calling them names and describing them as animals and less than human. The pattern is well documented and it has repeated itself again and again. While this book is not about the phenomena for dehumanisation, one can't but admit the power of stories which we tell ourselves about "us", the "others" and the world we occupy in making ordinary people do extraordinary things, both for better and worse.

Interestingly, we can, and should, play an active role in writing and directing our stories as some stories are more positive and more helpful than others. Happy, successful and achieved people tell themselves positive stories about the world and about their role in it. Their stories go along the lines of "I am full of capabilities, I can learn how to deal with different situations in life and people are essentially good and I can work with them to achieve our common goals. The world is full of resources and I can use those to add value and achieve success for myself and others." Compare this to a story like "I am not lucky and learning is always difficult for me. The world is full of people who want to take advantage over me." These stories could either help individuals achieve their potential or limit that potential altogether. These stories are behind our biggest successes as well as our major failures and conflicts.

Effective leaders not only tell themselves compelling stories about the world, but more importantly they can rally those with them around these stories. They have the ability to change the stories of the rest of us and through this they create a better future. The stories these effective leaders tell paint an uplifting future that we all can be part of. These stories even depict a world in which opportunities are abundant and learning takes place side by side by risk taking and failures. These stories and the positive mental habits they generate and cultivate impact the way a leader speaks, behaves and models the way, resulting in an embodied image of the desired state.

A Framework for Human Development and Performance

I hope now that we have established that the stories told by our left brain drive our behaviour to a large extent. Tell positive, empowering stories and this will be reflected in the way you engage with the world. The building blocks of our stories are the words we use, after all, language is what the left brain uses for its internal chatter. Noam Chomsky, the American linguist, philosopher, and cognitive scientist, believes that language evolved, primarily, as a mode of creating and interpreting thought. While language is used for communication, it is basically a system of thought and communication does not seem to be part of its design. According to Chomsky, "if you look carefully at the structure of language you will find case after case, right at the core of language design, where there is conflict between what would be efficient for communication and what is efficient for the specific biological design of language and in every case, that is known, communicative efficiency is sacrificed. It is just not a consideration. This conclusion has a widespread significance."

The framework proposed here is shown in the figure below. It resembles an iceberg, with the parts underwater driving and supporting the parts above.

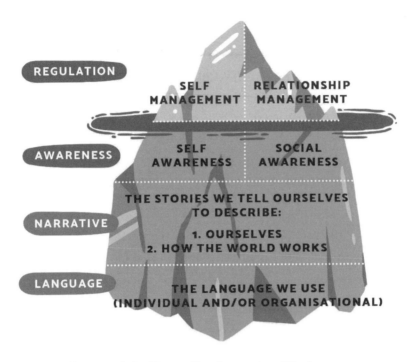

REGULATION

SELF MANAGEMENT | RELATIONSHIP MANAGEMENT

AWARENESS

SELF AWARENESS | SOCIAL AWARENESS

NARRATIVE

THE STORIES WE TELL OURSELVES TO DESCRIBE:

1. OURSELVES
2. HOW THE WORLD WORKS

LANGUAGE

THE LANGUAGE WE USE (INDIVIDUAL AND/OR ORGANISATIONAL)

Framework for Human Development and Performance

The different layers are described in the following sections.

Language

At the foundational level, we have the language we use and the words we choose. Here the language is viewed as a system of thoughts as described by Noam Chomsky. In this context, the avoidance of certain words is as important as the intentional use of others. The deliberate choice of the words and language feeding into the engine, which is the left brain; generates thoughts which is the bedrock of the human transformation and achievement. Individuals, educators and leaders will benefit from cultivating a positive and empowering language in themselves and those under their care and leadership. You may have noticed that successful and optimistic people who are having a positive impact on others often use highly energetic and positive language. We shall say more about the power of language when it comes to programming our minds in the next chapter.

Narrative and Stories

One day, a man and his three young children walked into a train station. The children were very playful and they went on annoying everyone at the station, endangering themselves as well as the other people. The father showed little interest in what the children were doing and did not attempt to restrain them. Clearly being an irresponsible father, many people grew frustrated with the situation as the children continued their dangerous and annoying horseplay.

What went through your mind while you read the paragraph above? Did you sympathise with the busy commuters and shared their frustration and concern for the safety of everyone including the children?

If so, you are not alone. Eventually, one commuter decided to intervene. The commuter approached the father and firmly told him "Sir! Don't you think you should try to control your children? We all are trying to get to our destinations safely here!" The father looked confused and politely answered "Yes. I guess you are right. I just don't know what to tell the children, I just came from the hospital and their mother just passed away a short while ago. I am really sorry, I just don't know what to do." Now what is going in your mind? If you are like most people, the feeling of frustration you felt earlier is replaced by feelings of sympathy and there may be even guilt for jumping into the wrong conclusion without giving the man the benefit of doubt. In both cases, you did not know all the details about what the man and his children are going through, and in both cases your left brain filled in the blanks and told you a story that drove your emotions and even the behaviour of the commuter who approached the father. That is how powerful the stories we tell ourselves are.

During a training session that was delivered to the academic staff at my university, I asked the participants to share achievements that they were able to attain because someone else believed in them. Many inspiring stories were shared, but I will always remember two stories shared by two members of staff. One of the lecturers shared that when she was a child; her father thought she was retarded. He treated her as one and she believed him! She was overwhelmed with emotions as she narrated that it was her mother, a lady that did not know how to read or write, who believed in her and told her that she can be whatever she wanted to be. The alternative story told by her mother propelled her to success. She ended up with a PhD in mechanical engineering; not bad for a retarded person!

Another lecturer said that when she was in primary school, she did not like school at all. She confessed that she used to put a storybook inside her schoolbooks and pretend to study while, in reality, she was reading her stories. One day, her teacher called her mother to give her feedback. Making sure that the child was listening, the teacher told the mother that her daughter had really beautiful handwriting. Our colleague said, "that statement totally changed my relationship with the school, I really wanted to impress my teacher." That same little girl now has a PhD in chemical engineering.

We can never underestimate the impact of stories we tell ourselves about ourselves, others and how the world works, on our success and how we carry ourselves and manage our relationships with other people. In the framework described here, the stories layer is right on top of the language layer. While the language we use and the language surrounding us powers our stories, the evolution of these stories is not a simple process as many parties contribute to directing them. This ranges from the media to our friends, parents and teachers.

When teachers teach their students about the world and encourage them to pursue their dreams, achieve their full potential and learn how to live peacefully with others, these teachers are, in essence, trying to change and improve the stories their students are telling in their minds. When businesses or sales people bombard us with advertisement in the media about their products and services, they want us to tell ourselves stories in which these products or services represent important things for us. And when politicians campaign, they want to change our stories and adopt their political views as the way the world works.

Just like stories told in the minds of individuals, communities and organisations have their own stories too. These stories are told through culture, folklore, legends, traditions as well as vision and mission statements. The collective and common stories that are told by groups of people, especially large ones, are essential for these groups to work and operate effectively. In groups where people do not personally know each other, common narratives and shared stories about these groups that promote trust and the sense of identity and belonging represent an important social glue. In a nation for example, very few know the president in person, but collectively, the nation tells a story about her or him and how did she or he ascend to power. The same can be said about other national aspects from economic and political systems to the constitution, they are the stories that groups of people opt to collectively tell, respect and accept as important basis for the national existence.

For example, I recently purchased a microwave oven online. I did not know who sold it to me but when I punched in my credit card number I trusted that the microwave will be delivered in due course. Sure enough, in two days I received the parcel in good condition. Trust in the economic system emerges when enough people "believe" in it. It is a story that we tell together. We trust banks with our money because the story we all tell ourselves is that "when we want our money, the bank will give it back to us, plus interest." When this story is shaken, like what happened in Greece recently, when people started to have doubts whether the banks will give them their money, there was a run on the bank. Whatever applies to nations can be applied to other human groups such as tribes, teams, schools and companies.

Awareness

We are not always aware of what is going on in our minds and in the minds of those around us. That's why having self-awareness of our stories, thoughts and feelings, and social awareness of the stories, emotions and relationships around us represent an important link between the mental processes that take place in the mind and how our outlook is represented to the world.

The awareness layer is a very important one as it plays the role of a filter between the stories and the behaviour. Aware individuals, for example, will reject the language and stories that dehumanise others which will in turn make stereotyping and ill treatment of others more unlikely. Awareness of the stories told by individuals allow them the opportunity to edit and direct these stories in the most positive and productive way.

Regulation

Ultimately the visible part of how we engage the world is manifested by how we manage ourselves and our relationships. The roles that self-management and relationship management play in our success and happiness cannot be underestimated.

It is to be noted that the awareness and regulation layers discussed above mimic the emotional intelligence framework developed by Daniel Goleman and they will be discussed later in the book, in details, within this context.

THE STORIES

We become the stories we tell ourselves. So we need to be careful what stories are we telling.

Our stories become our identities and realities, individual and organisational.

Research shows that there are

Groups who tell collective stories can work together and collaborate.

These are team charters, organisational mission and visions and national values.

2 TYPES OF MINDSETS*

Our brains create a representation of the world inside them, we call these mindsets. Adopting a mindset is a choice.

Fixed Mindset

Those with Fixed Mindset tell themselves a story about success being a result of innate capabilities that cannot be changed. When they fail, they get frustrated and give up.

CHOOSE THIS

Growth Mindset

Those who choose to adopt Growth Mindset tell themselves a story that success is governed by attitude and the willingness to put the necessary effort, rather than innate capabilities only. When they are faced with obstacles or when they fail, they view this as part of the learning and keep on trying."

*As described by CAROL DWEK

Human Development

A FRAMEWORK FOR INDIVIDUAL AND ORGANISATIONAL CHANGE

The language we use powers the stories we tell ourselves.

Through awareness of our language, stories and emotions we can manage ourselves and our relationships better. This can lead to success and happiness.

Sustainable Change & Human development & Motivation

REGULATION

| SELF MANAGEMENT | RELATIONSHIP MANAGEMENT |

AWARENESS

| SELF AWARENESS | SOCIAL AWARENESS |

NARRATIVE

THE STORIES WE TELL OURSELVES TO DESCRIBE:

1. OURSELVES
2. HOW THE WORLD WORKS

LANGUAGE

THE LANGUAGE WE USE (INDIVIDUAL AND/OR ORGANISATIONAL)

If we want a sustainable positive change and human development, we need to begin by changing the language we use, telling different stories and developing awareness as well as regulate ourselves and our relationships.

Shoot the Boss!

(This page is intentionally left blank)

3

How to Program a Mind

"The limits of my language means the limits of my world."

Ludwig Wittgenstein

Have you ever tried to watch a YouTube video only to be greeted by a pre-roll ad that you cannot skip? YouTube makes money from advertisements by forcing you to watch the first 5 seconds of an ad with the hope that you will remain interested to watch the rest of it. Majority of us will wait impatiently to click the "Skip Ad" button and this represents a major challenge to advertising agencies. Ogilvy Cape Town is a South African advertising agency that decided to transform this challenge into an opportunity when they worked on a pre-roll ad for the Audi R8. The ad focuses on only one feature of the car, its ability to accelerate from 0 to 100 km/h in less than 3.5 seconds. The ad shows the car speeding up while the screen indicates both the speed and the time lapsed. Once the 100 km/h and 3.5 second marks are reached, the screen turns black with the massage "You can skip the ad now." Thinking about it, this is a truly remarkable and a memorable way to advertise the car. This was possible mainly because the creators of the ad were able to reframe the situation and tell a different story, seeing the limited time available as an opportunity rather than a challenge.

Gone in 5 seconds Audi R8 ad.

In the rest of this chapter we will discuss how we can use language to systematically reframe situations positively and develop mental habits to tell more useful, motivating and effective stories.

Language and Thinking

We mentioned earlier that Noam Chomsky postulated that language evolved, primarily, as a mode of creating and interpreting thought. We shall continue to explore and establish the relationship between language, thinking and the stories we tell. It is also interesting to note here that computer science has contributed a fair share of our current understanding of how thinking takes place. Just like the human brain, we do use language to programme our computers. Computer programming languages are used to manipulate different variables in the computer programme. Before the computer can process a variable, the variable is required to be declared or named. This is like giving the variable a birth certificate and a location at the memory of the computer. This process is followed by classifying the variable or stating its type. A computer variable can be classified as real, integer or character, for example. Once a variable is named and classified, the programme can process it. A number of theories have been put forward to describe how thinking takes place and my favourite theory is the one that elucidates the role of language in the formation of thoughts. This theory is very briefly described below and it has implications on how we learn and communicate. Similar to computer programming, thinking and learning happen in three stages:

1. Naming (labelling)
2. Classifying
3. Processing

In order for the brain to store and process ideas, thoughts and concepts, the brain starts by assigning these concepts names. We do that all the time, whenever we are faced with a novel situation or when we meet new people, the brain needs to give them names in order to process them. If we meet someone and we do not know that person's name, we may use a feature of the person as a name. If the person is tall, we may name him the tall man, if she is not from this country, we may name her the foreign lady and so on. This facilitates the storage part of the thinking. This naming stage is very important and it is fuelled by the language we use. It will also have an impact on how the whole thinking process will unfold.

Now, if we are to have an interest in the person, object or the concept, our brain shall attach some classification to it. This classification could be anything like good, bad, hot, bitter, difficult, etc. In other words, a story is told about what we have just named with the intention of integrating the new knowledge or information into the existing narrative and making sense of the whole thing. This is accompanied by electrochemical activity in the neurons (firing) which will result in initiating neuronal connections in the brain to process the new concept. The interesting thing about this theory is that it provides some control over the entire process of thinking through altering the naming and classifying stages.

Let me illustrate this with an example that I use when I deliver my training sessions. When I show a picture of a cockroach and ask the audience to name it, all of them will say that it is a cockroach. So, this is the naming stage. When I ask them what they think of it, most of them say things like dirty, disgusting, ugly, etc. This is the classifying stage. This reflects the mental models and stories that are normally told about this creature which is one of the international symbols of disgust. Now when the audience are asked of what should be done with the cockroach, majority will recommend destroying it because they are 'wired' to do so.

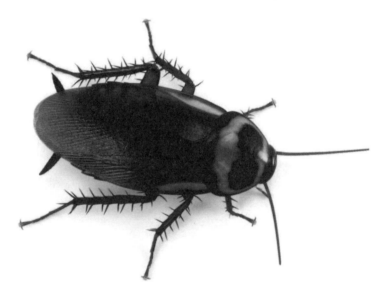

A Cockroach. (Source: www.kaneexterminating.com)

After explaining the thinking theory, I show the picture of the cockroach again and ask the audience to name it without using any negative terms. This implies not using the term "cockroach" as it has many negative connotations already. One suggestion is to use its scientific name *Blattaria*. This is a fresh name with no classification attached. Now the audience is asked to describe the Blattaria using positive or neutral terms. This is done to use positive language to invoke more positive stories. Sure enough, suggestions like 6-legged, brown, flyer, resourceful, flexible, protein rich and even "roommate" start to emerge. When I ask, "what should we do with it?", an apparent shift in the mind of the audience is present and they are not necessarily recommending destruction anymore. Clearly, using different naming and classifying terms creates new stories and brain patterns that are wired through training and repetition, and this how learning takes place.

This can have an immediate positive impact on our capacity to develop new positive mental habits that can help us conceive solutions to the challenges we face and engage with the world more optimistically. We have institutionalised this at the university where I was the dean of engineering. We outlawed the use of the P-word (probelm) and replaced it wherever it appears in our language, and in the curriculum, with the word "opportunity." The same deal is made with everyone who takes my Massive Open Online Courses (MOOCs). To encourage our students and staff to stop using the P-word, we created what we call the "Opportunity Note." Modelled after a Dollar, I give each one of my students an Opportunity Note at the beginning of my courses, if they keep their promise of not using the P-word throughout the semester, I will personally sign the Opportunity Note for them. I have also mailed Opportunity Notes around the world to my online students. Clearly, I do not have a way to watch my students 24/7 but creating a physical object (the Opportunity Note) makes the word come to life. As more students report great and enjoyable experiences, the stories and culture continue to take root. The Opportunity Note is shown below and I would like to recommend that you start removing the P-word from your vocabulary and begin to influence your stories and thinking process at the naming stage.

The Opportunity Note

Now, when I speak about using language to redirect our narrative and create a more positive mindset, I offer the audience the opportunity to have an Opportunity Note each and make a pledge not to use the P-word. This ritualises the whole process and makes an even stronger impact. The pictures below show different groups taking the pledge.

Students from Dundee University and Heriot-Watt University posing with their Opportunity Notes

Medical students from the National University Malaysia (UKM) pledging not to use the P-word

Deborah Ramirez displayed her commitment to eradicating the P-word by putting a sign that reads "Say No to the P Word" on the rear windscreen of her car, turning heads and creating conversations around the role of positive language wherever she goes. We will read more about her story later in the book.

Say No to the P-Word

A number of students in my Massive Open Online Course (MOOC) reported how using language to reframe their stories helped them in different contexts.

Humaira Ansari, a clinical hypnotherapist from Manchester, UK commented that "Stripping off the P-word of its power by replacing it with the word 'opportunity' has been one of the most useful methods I use with my clients, helping them unlock their unlimited potential within and overcome any stuck-ness they may experience."

Asma Harb from San Francisco, USA said "Replacing the 'P-Word' with the word 'Opportunity' has made magic in my life! I have become a more focused, more organised and more determined person with the brilliant thought in my mind that I can make a real change and I can always challenge any obstacle and probelm I face in my life and turn them into new opportunities!"

Ferial Fakier, a participant from Australia said "I am a healthcare practitioner, practicing for 7 years before I joined a global healthcare equipment company in sales and marketing. There is almost a natural tendency to be negative in an environment where income is driven by sales, meeting targets and extended hours of travel. After challenging myself to exclude the P-word in my daily vocabulary, constantly adjusting my mindset to be positive, and proactively acknowledging my emotions, my colleagues have noticed a change in me.

"I then started noticing a boomerang effect on my team and the people around me, a positive energy that I was giving off was now always bouncing back at me. I liked this!!

"I then challenged the team I work with to exclude the P-word from their vocabulary as well, it was now some sort of game we were playing. We have incorporated words like solutions, pivot points, obstacles, some people have given it a whole new perspective and it is quite humorous. I recall some colleagues calling out 'my situation needs healing' and 'we can Band-Aid that'.

"This concept in my team is still at teething phase but I've already seen some positive changes in the team, a point where we all are committed to thinking of positive outcomes and assessing our personal emotions towards challenging situations." Ferial concluded.

Lao Tzu once said, "Watch your thoughts, they become words. Watch your words, they become actions. Watch your actions, they become habits. Watch your habits, they become character. Watch your character, it becomes your destiny."

It is worth noting that in some languages, like Arabic, there are two different words to represent the English word "probelm", "Mushkilah" is the Arabic word for probelm as a source of trouble or worry; and "Masaalah" is the translation of probelm as a question raised for intellectual enquiry. Replacing the word "probelm" with "opportunity" is aimed at creating mental habits of seeing all probelms as solutions in disguise that require unearthing and discovering.

Knocking a man out with one punch, also referred to as a "king hit," was causing an increasing number of casualties in Australia. In July 2012, a "king hit" caused the death of Thomas Kelly. Another victim, Daniel Christie, was in a critical condition after receiving a "king hit" on New Year's Eve of 2014. This has sparked a debate about the use of the term "king hit" which seems to glorify violence. Some activists together with the family of Daniel Christie are suggesting to change the term from a "king hit" to a "coward's punch." This renaming is meant to deprive this act of violence from the glory which its current name lends. Mike Gallacher, the NSW State Police Minister agreed with this proposal and encouraged the community and media to use the term "coward's punch" instead to help embarrass and shame offenders.

Words represent the materials of our thoughts. In order for us to be able to intellectually engage objects, persons, behaviours or phenomena, they will need to have names that describe them first. For example, a relatively new paradox is that as the world gets more connected, individuals grew more disconnected to those physically close to them, this is exemplified by behaviours that are still new that they do not have names attached to them, such as ignoring the person in front of you in favour of your smart phone. Perhaps this lack of naming is the reason why we are not able to address this challenge effectively! In May 2012, a group of people were determined to change this. They gathered at the University of Sydney in Australia and among them was a lexicologist, a phonetician, a debating champion, a poet, authors and a cruciverbalist (a professional crossword maker). They suggested the word "phubbing" (a combination of phone and snubbing) to describe "the act of holding a mobile phone in a social setting of two or more people, and then interacting with that mobile phone and not the people in that setting." Now we have a word to describe the behaviour, we can say things like "stop phubbing me!" or "don't be a phubber," or even "#SayNoToPhubbing."

We live in a world that is made of our words. People can make our day by saying a nice word to us and similarly, hearing a harsh word can spoil our moods for a long time. The thinking model of naming-classifying-processing is an invitation to cultivate a language that facilitates the realisation of opportunities as well as success, happiness, and potential fulfilment for everyone involved.

It is established that the human brain creates a representation of the world in order for us to mentally deal with the world. Stories play a central role in this representation and renaming existing concepts in this representation can assist in the reframing of situations. Just like renaming a P-word as an opportunity or the cockroach as "blattaria," if we would like to improve a relationship with a "difficult" colleague, one way is to start by renaming that colleague, in our minds, so instead of calling her or him the "difficult person," we may pick a trait of the person that is more positive and declare that as the new name!

It is necessary here to mention that renaming of situations, people and objects to reframe situations and initiate positive development is not akin to encouraging people to be in denial. On the contrary, it is an active and creative approach to channel the energy positively towards creating a different reality.

In 2013, the 34-year-old Alex Lewis was leading a normal life in the city of Stockbridge in the UK. He ran his own business successfully until he contracted streptococcal infection, a disease that resulted in the amputation of his arms, legs, nose and even lips. One could only imagine how difficult and distressing the situation was to Mr Lewis and his family, however, amazingly Alex told the BBC that "the year I lost my limbs was the most brilliant of my life." He did not describe the year as "difficult" or "challenging" but "the most brilliant." By creating a positive narrative, Alex could cope better with what he is facing. He sure did not wish that he lost his limbs, but now that he is a quadriplegic amputee, he needs to make the best out of the deal. He opted to focus on the love and support that his family and friends offered him as well as the fact that he was still alive and able to support his family. His positivity was a necessary ingredient in his recovery and rehabilitation. After fitting him with prosthetic legs, Alex started a 10-week walking course, but he surprised everybody as he was walking again within two weeks.

The Brain, Learning and Mindset

Two seriously ill men shared a room at a hospital. One of them had a bed that was closer to the only window in the room. Every afternoon, for an hour, the man was made to sit up to drain the fluid in his lungs. The window overlooked a beautiful park with a nice lake. Children played with their model boats and lovers walked holding hands while the sun reflected over the surface of the lake. The man closer to the window kept describing what happens in the park to his fellow patient who was always looking forward to that time of the day when he knows what happens in the world just outside the hospital. He closes his eyes and allows the visions of happiness and beauty to fill his mind. One day there was a parade in the park and while he was unable to hear the sound of the music, he listened to the vivid descriptions coming from his friend close to the window and he was able to see the parade in all its detail. The days went by and one day the nurse bringing the morning medication was confronted by the lifeless body of the man near the window. The body was removed and the remaining patient indicated his interest in moving his bed closer to the window. His wish was granted. Once settled down, the man painfully sat up and looked through the window. To his surprise, he found that the window was facing just another wall! Puzzled, the man asked the nurse when was the wall erected and where is the park his late friend used to describe to him daily. The nurse was really surprised as she explained not only that the wall has always been there, but that the dead friend was blind!

I bet that as you read the description of the lake and the park, just like the other man in the hospital, you could almost hear the music and see the sunlight reflected on the surface of the lake. As discussed earlier, the brain works through generating stories and mental models that impose order on chaos and deduce patterns to compare with previous experiences, impacting the way we perceive ourselves, others and interpret the world around us. Faced with the same reality, different people have different mental models, and that is why we perceive the same events differently drawing different meanings from them. For example, if two individuals are learning how to play a violin and both of them struggle equally with their learning, that struggle is nothing but an event that is happening to both of them as they push the limits of what they are capable of. Now each individual will use his or her mental models to interpret this event (the struggle). One mental model may be "playing the violin needs more practice; if I persevere long enough, I will be able to play beautiful musical pieces in due course". Another mental model may be "this is difficult for me. I do not have the talent for music; I will never be able to learn how to play the violin." It is clear how each mental model will drive each individual on a totally different path.

Decades of research in human motivation indicate that its main source is our search for meaning. We are positive, motivated and on top of our game when we work on something that is meaningful to us. To achieve this, it is important to continue training and rewiring our brains to develop the muscles of positive thinking that are necessary to view challenges as opportunities so that we can, through them, create a better world.

The collection of mental models that we myelinate and cultivate result in our overall mindset and attitudes that drive how we perceive the world, our role in that world, and how we respond to the challenges we encounter. When confronted with a new situation, one individual may see adversity, while another may see opportunity, depending on the mental model that they adopt.

Entrepreneurship, innovation and creativity are simply mental models that are adopted by individuals. Entrepreneurial, innovative, creative and highly motivated individuals cultivate the ability to generate positive mental models that are crafted to see opportunities in any new situation. Being able to see the opportunity even in adversity is literally the ability to generate positive and flexible mental models to see the world through.

Growth Mindset

In the book *Mindset*, Carol Dweck described two types of mindset. The first she called "fixed mindset" which is held by individuals who believe that the capabilities that they have are fixed by their genes. The second type is "growth mindset" which reflects a narrative that describes capabilities and skills as things that can be learnt and developed, provided sufficient commitment and effort are dedicated for that. We can say that the mindset is the story we tell and probably you have guessed that those with growth mindset are more capable of developing themselves and adding value to themselves and those around them. The role of leaders and educators is to encourage others to adopt the growth mindset. [1]

In his book, *Outliers*, Malcolm Gladwell studied a number of high performing individuals including Bill Gates and Tiger Woods. He concluded that to achieve mastery level in a major competitive discipline such as sport, art, science or business, individuals need to dedicate around 10,000 hours of focused practice and training. This level of commitment and consistency is definitely an indication of the growth mindset. Whenever we see a master performing, we are tempted to think that the master is talented and lucky to be able to perform at that level. The fact of the matter is that mastery is always a product of a mindset that sees the struggle in new challenges as a stepping-stone towards progress and high performance. This is true for golf, chess, physics or music. All masters practice their craft religiously, building and strengthening myelin layers over the neurocircuits that they have cultivated over repeated and conscious practice. We are not saying here that talent or physical traits do not play a role, undoubtedly if you are taller than average, for example, you will have a better chance at excelling in basketball. The argument here is that talent is not sufficient for mastery. [2]

To be successful in life and work, the ability to develop positive stories and mental models is paramount. Developing these positive stories and mental models requires committing the time and effort to practice and learn necessitating many sacrifices on the way.

There is enough evidence that we can exert control over what habits, stories and mental models we form through repetition, reflection, willpower and intentional thinking as well as the use of experienced coaches and mentors. These intentional mental activities cause myelin growth and strengthen the neuron connections, literally hardwiring the mental models we are inculcating. Through this we are able to nurture positive mental models that will support growth, development and learning. The collections of mental models that we maintain will, literally, create our world and form our mindset.

Nurturing positive growth-inclined stories and mindset is very necessary for success both professionally and in life at large. Individuals who continuously develop their mindset are lifelong learners who will be able to fulfil their full potential and play a key role in helping others achieve their full potential as well. In order to be effective individuals who can develop people, products and systems that make life worth living and support the increasing population of our planet, it is important that we develop a positive attitude and see the world as full of opportunities and cultivate mental habits to construct mental models that enable us to spot those opportunities and create value out of them. Here we need to reiterate that our perception of reality is extremely important. Strictly speaking, there is no absolute reality, and that is why two individuals facing the same situation may end up seeing adversity or opportunity depending on their mental model.

Studying the biographies of successful individuals, who managed to have a lasting impact on those around them, seem to suggest a formula or a process for success. This formula seems to imply that success happens when we work on something that we are interested in and are willing to commit our time and effort towards. Interest and commitment, when coupled with the right practicing technique, coaching and feedback for improvement, will result in achieving mastery and success. These elements are discussed below.

Interest

The journey to success starts with interest, successful people often pursue goals that they are interested in and are in alignment with their life purpose. Nudging life goals and the inner narratives towards each other will enable the left brain to continue weaving the coherent meaningful story of our existence allowing us to create meaning. Simon Sinek calls this "start with why". In his book carrying the same title, he cited many examples of organisations and individuals from Martin Luther King to Apple Inc. where successful and inspirational leaders are very clear of the "why", the reason for their existence, and use that to communicate and inspire. It is important for individuals and organisations that seek success, happiness and fulfilment to articulate their interests and life purposes as this is the key to sustaining them throughout the ups and downs of the life journey. Writing down a "Vision" statement, for both individuals and organisations, is a worthwhile effort in this direction. If done right, it can bring a lot of clarity to answer the existential question "what is the purpose of our existence?" [3]

Commitment

Pursuing what interests us is an essential starting point but it is not sufficient for success. We need to be committed to allocate the time and effort necessary to build the success mindset. Willingness to push the limit and operate outside our comfort zone is a prerequisite for honing new skills and attitudes leading towards success. Interestingly, that willingness to explore uncharted territories is also the reason why we will inevitably fail before we achieve mastery. This "failure" is a necessary feedback that we should use to know what to change and where to improve in order to fare better next time. The way we respond to failure is a very good indication of the depth of our interest in what we are pursuing and it represents a reflection of our mindsets and the stories we tell ourselves as well. It is necessary that we cultivate awareness to the story we tell ourselves when we are faced with difficulties so that we can nudge the story in a positive and useful trajectory. An interested committed mindset will perceive failure as getting us a step closer to success through uncovering shortcomings and things to change.

It is necessary here to mention that the definition of failure in this section, and most of the book, is the inability to achieve the desired results when we push the limit of what we are capable of or what the current paradigms allow. This failure often yields very positive learning that can be used to further improve performance in the future.

Practicing Technique, Coaching and Feedback

Techniques are mental frameworks that we use to improve our performance while pursuing our developmental goals. Often these techniques are used under the tutelage of a coach, teacher, mentor or a master of some sort. Techniques refer to the way sportswomen and sportsmen train when they prepare for the Olympics, for example. The presence of a coach is often very important. I taught myself swimming at the age of 27. I had the interest and I was truly committed. I went to the swimming pool every day and watched how other people swam. Eventually, I was able to swim, but my technique is not good at all. I attribute this to the fact that I did not get someone to show me how to do it right and provide me with timely feedback so that I can correct and alter my technique and build myelin around the right brain circuitry.

The practice that leads to success takes place with full awareness on the part of the trainee while a selected limit is being pushed. For example, when a runner is trying to break her own record, she may try a new rhythm of running or breathing. As she tries this new breathing technique, her performance may take a dip, she needs to be aware of what is happening in her body and mind, and continue practicing, fine tuning and perfecting the skill. When a limit is pushed, any failure is a feedback or symptom that indicates that further fine tuning is necessary, so failure should be expected, accepted and even welcomed as a sign that we are on the path to enhance and improve the skill.

How to Craft Habits and Mindsets

It is clear now that formation of mental models is a process that happens over time as myelin grows along the neuronal pathways. We have a choice of allowing this process to take place unconsciously or to take charge of it and literally use myelin to craft our desired mindset. This section proposes three main techniques to growing a positive mindset, brain rewiring, language and thinking, as a mental model.

We mentioned earlier that mental models to recognise danger exist much earlier in the evolution of the brain as they can be a necessary prerequisite for survival. However, mental models that recognise opportunities can be inculcated. One exercise that can be used to improve our capability to see the positive side of events is brain rewiring, this is where we purposefully record 5 things that we are grateful for on a daily basis. Students who took my courses were required to perform brain rewiring daily and by the end of the semester, most of them reported increased capability to see opportunities in their lives. This is going to be discussed in more detail in the following chapters dedicated to emotional intelligence.

Change Management

The framework described in this book can be used to inform and guide transformation and change management process too. Often the goal of change management is to transform and change behaviour at an individual, team, organisational, national or even global level. This may take the shape of becoming more health conscious (individual), communicate openly (team) or becoming more customer focused (organisation), transform the educational system (national), or even reversing climate change (global). Time after time change management efforts fall short of achieving their targets because they focus on changing the behaviour, through extrinsic motivations, without transforming the language and the narrative.

A more sustainable approach to change management happens when the strategies adopted to enact the desirable change are orchestrated at all levels, starting with language, introducing new narratives and developing awareness of that narrative leading towards the more desirable behaviour which can be supported with a reward scheme.

Simon Sinek, the bestselling author of *Start with Why* said that when he first started speaking to large audiences he felt nervous, noticing that the body reacts in similar ways when nervous and when excited, Simon started telling himself that he is excited, before he goes on stage. This made a huge difference in the way he behaved and delivered his highly-acclaimed presentations.

The same can be said when transforming businesses, organisations and even nations. While redirecting the use of resources, information, business processes and budgetary allocations are very important to organisational change management, a sustainable change ought to be accompanied, if not led, by a change of organisational language and organisational narrative. More about this in the coming chapters.

LANGUAGE, BRAIN & THE MIND

We live in a world that is made out of our words.

LANGUAGE PROGRAMMING

1. Naming: Cockroach
2. Classifying: Bad, Dirty
3. Processing: Kill it

The brain is the most complex object in the known universe.

It is also a very powerful computer. Computers are programed using programming languages, so is the brain.

USE POSITIVE LANGUAGE!

Cockroach → Blattaria ✓

Enemy → Potential Partner ✓

Pledge to replace the P-WORD with the word OPPORTUNITY in your language.

1 OPPORTUNITY

Use the Opportunity Note to gamify the concept and remind yourself of not using the P-word.

Its fun when done with others!

Shoot the Boss!

(This page is intentionally left blank)

4

Success and Emotional Intelligence

"If your emotional abilities aren't in hand, if you don't have self-awareness, if you are not able to manage your distressing emotions, if you can't have empathy and have effective relationships, then no matter how smart you are, you are not going to get very far."

Daniel Goleman

"We cannot tell what may happen to us in the strange medley of life. But we can decide what happens in us, how we can take it, what we do with it, and that is what really counts in the end."

Joseph Fort Newton

Humans are the most successful species on earth. For better or worse, we control the world we live in. There exist a number of explanations to why are we more successful than other animals. However, Yuval Harari, the author of *Sapiens*, attributes this success to our ability to collaborate flexibly in large numbers. While large number collaborative behaviour is exhibited by other species such as ants and bees, the collaboration exhibited by these species is rigid and limited in context. "If a beehive is facing a new threat or a new opportunity, the bees cannot reinvent their social system overnight in order to cope better. They cannot, for example, execute the queen and establish a republic." Harari said [1]. Other species may hunt collaboratively which requires working flexibly together, but this often happens in small, tightly knit groups. The main reason behind this unique human success is our ability to tell, and believe, collective stories about our teams, tribes, organisations and nations. When we collectively believe in our economic system, legal system and political system, we can collaborate with those having the same belief, even if we do not know them in person. We can trade and exchange services because we believe that we will be paid for the work we did and that the money we will receive is accepted by others when we want to exchange it for what we want, we believe that banks will give us back our money upon request and when our rights are breached, we can go to the authorities and ask for help.

So clearly, at more levels than one, our success is dependent on our ability to trust each other and work collaboratively in large groups. The quality of the relationships that we are in does not only determine how successful we are, it determine how happy and healthy we are too! In the interconnected world we are living in today, the notion of relationship extends to our relationships with the environment we live in and our responsibility to other species.

Emotional intelligence begins with self-awareness which is the awareness of our own emotions, existence and our role in the bigger scheme of things as well as the impact we have on our surroundings and others. Emotional Intelligence extends to how can we build successful and thriving relationships with others. In a nutshell, possessing high levels of emotional intelligence results in nurturing good relationships with others, including our loved ones, customers, work colleagues, superiors and even the natural environment we exist within, and this, inevitably will make us happy, healthy and successful.

Recently, the concept of emotional intelligence began to attract the attention of educationalists, business leaders and policy makers. There is a huge opportunity to integrate emotional intelligence systematically into the education system so that individuals are given the opportunity to develop these essential skills through a holistic education. Holistic education and human development are integrated processes that aim not only at developing skills necessary for employment, but also at ensuring the emotional well-being of individuals. This often is referred to as training the head, heart, and hands. The good news is that the only part of the body that we need to train is the brain! Knowledge, emotions and even manual skills are all cultivated, developed and stored in the brain. The integrated holistic development of knowledge, skills, and emotional competencies will result in individuals who are not only ready for employment but also ready for life's challenges through being resilient, purpose-driven individuals who can fulfil their full human potential and help others achieve the same. Purpose-driven individuals have a positive growth mindset that gives them a belief that they can have a positive impact on life. This motivation is a necessary prerequisite for approaching work and life positively.

While the emotional intelligence sections of this book draw on the writings of Daniel Goleman, especially *Emotional Intelligence* [2] and *Working with Emotional Intelligence* [3], these sections are not intended as a replacement for reading Goleman's excellent books, in fact, I highly recommend them. As mentioned earlier, I taught a free Massive Open Online Course (MOOC) called *Success with Emotional Intelligence* to more than 5000 students. Participants from all over the world found the tools I introduced useful and to complement the theoretical framework described by Daniel Goleman.

I measured the emotional intelligence of the students who attended my course and compared it to that of a control group. The measurement happened twice, at the beginning of the semester, when the course was offered, and at the end of it. To infer the level of their emotional intelligence, students were asked to complete a detailed questionnaire. The results were very encouraging with the students who completed the 18-week course achieving growth in all aspects of the emotional intelligence compared to the control group. In this chapter I will attempt to introduce the concept of emotional intelligence from a big picture point of view to prepare us for more detailed examination over the following chapters.

What is Intelligence?

Intelligence is a widely-used word but we seldom stop and ask ourselves what it means. It has been defined in a variety of ways that are related to cognitive capacities in humans. Intelligence has been observed in nature and other living creatures as well. Artificial intelligence is the capacity that is programmed into machines (computers) enabling them to respond to new situations and learn. Intelligence can refer to the mental ability to think, learn, recognise patterns, logically predict outcomes, and respond to a variety of stimuli. Steven Pinker, the author of *How the Mind Works*, defines intelligence as the ability to attain goals in the face of obstacles by means of decisions based on rational (truth-obeying) rules. Intelligence Quotient (IQ) is the measure of the ability to comprehend logical, geometrical, and mathematical challenges [4]. While IQ is a useful indication of future success, the challenges of the 21st century increasingly need other kinds of intelligence that IQ does not measure. Historically what made humans special, when compared to other creatures and even intelligent machines, is the high intelligence and consciousness. Interestingly, the last few decades resulted in the creation of highly intelligent machines that were able to beat humans at the game of intelligence. On 10 February 1996, Deep Blue, a chess playing computer designed by IBM, defeated Gary Kasparov, the chess world champion. Since then, more and more machines are getting better at doing intelligent work that used to be considered as exclusively in the human domain. In all likelihood, this trend will continue and it will have a large impact on the nature of work that humans will be doing. With more jobs being automated and being done by machines, we need to cultivate skills and mindsets that will allow us to remain relevant in the world.

Interestingly, with all the progress that was done with machine intelligence, very little advancement happened in the realm of artificial consciousness. As consciousness and the emotional domains remain strictly human-centred, perhaps these will be the areas to focus on to future proof ourselves as technological developments change the way we live. This will go hand in hand in developing higher order thinking skills.

As explained in the previous chapters, the brain has three main regions, the old brain, which is dedicated to survival instincts; the middle brain, where emotions are processed; and the new brain, where rational high level thinking happens. We perceive the world around us through the variety of sensory signals that are relayed to our brains. Signals flow in and out of the brain through its lower part, the old and middle brain; which means that any signal that goes through the brain will be emotionally "flavoured" before reaching the new brain for rational processing. This is the reason we sometimes emotionally overreact to events and stimuli. Being aware of this emotional overdrive and being able to manage the impact of emotions on ourselves as well as others around us is called Emotional Intelligence.

Surviving and thriving in the 21st century, which is a key century that is riddled with grand challenges for the humanity as a whole, requires holistic development of individuals in both the cognitive and emotional domains. This is a prerequisite for nations' competitiveness, prosperity and security. Despite the wide realisation that national education systems ought to be geared towards the provision of holistic education, there is a gap between this realisation and what happens in reality at schools and universities around the world. In his book, the *Global Achievement Gap*, Tony Wagner identified 7 survival skills for the 21st century that, according to him, are not systematically developed in schools today [5]. These skills are:

1. Critical thinking

2. Collaboration across networks
3. Agility and adaptability
4. Initiative and entrepreneurialism
5. Effective oral and written communication
6. Accessing and analysing information
7. Curiosity and imagination

It is clear that in order to maintain nations' competitiveness and achieve holistic development of individuals and societies, it is paramount to adopt an integrated approach to inculcating both IQ and Emotional Intelligence, leading towards the development of human capital equipped with all the necessary survival skills.

Emotional Intelligence

Deep inside our hearts (or should I say brains!), we are all ultimately chasing happiness. We may be seeking success in the form of money or power, we may be seeking status or fulfilment, but if we dig deeper, often happiness is what we find as our fundamental motive. Now, happiness is not easily defined either, as it means different things to different people. The definition I like is that happiness is the quality of one's relationships. If you think about it, after achieving the basics in life, such as having health, food, shelter, what really matters is how good are our relationships with our loved ones, students, teachers, co-workers, fellow drivers on the road, and almost everyone else. Collaboration and teamwork, which are key success skills in today's work, school, and life in general, are also functions of the quality of relationships that we are able to cultivate and develop with others. Emotional intelligence is an essential ingredient for nurturing healthy and productive relationships. It is the skill and ability to understand, recognise, predict and appropriately respond to emotions in one's self and in others, as well as in groups and teams. Daniel Goleman presented a neat and useful framework to describe the four aspects of emotional intelligence, namely self-awareness, social awareness, self-management and relationship management [2]. The framework,

66

together with a description of its main aspects, is discussed further in the following chapters.

It is clear that Goleman's emotional intelligence framework sits within the wider framework of human development and performance described in chapter 2 which has 4 layers, the language, the narratives, the awareness and the regulation. The last two layers are the emotional intelligence part.

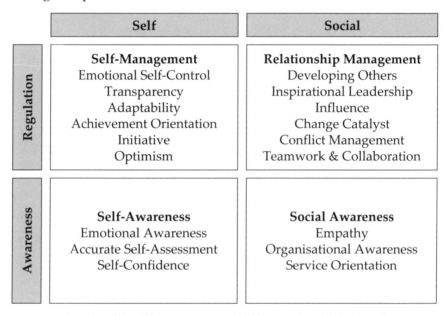

	Self	Social
Regulation	**Self-Management** Emotional Self-Control Transparency Adaptability Achievement Orientation Initiative Optimism	**Relationship Management** Developing Others Inspirational Leadership Influence Change Catalyst Conflict Management Teamwork & Collaboration
Awareness	**Self-Awareness** Emotional Awareness Accurate Self-Assessment Self-Confidence	**Social Awareness** Empathy Organisational Awareness Service Orientation

Emotional Intelligence Framework. (Source: Daniel Goleman)

The Business Case for Emotional Intelligence

Besides achieving wellbeing and health, and these are no trivial things to attain, scientific evidences points towards the finding that emotional intelligence is good for the bottom line. Coupled with the widely-accepted view that it is possible to develop and improve one's emotional intelligence skills through training, intentional use of language and positive habits inculcation, this should be good news. Businesses and organisations around the world from the US Airforce to L'Oreal are seeing the benefits of either recruiting emotionally intelligent individuals or even supporting the development of emotional intelligence traits within their people.

Happiness Index

Not only businesses are recognising the importance of emotional intelligence, wellbeing and happiness, but nations too. As a matter of fact, the Kingdom of Bhutan was ahead of the game in recognising the importance of promoting and measuring happiness earlier than many corporate players. Bhutan is a small country in the Himalayas. While nations traditionally measure their performance using the Gross Domestic Product (GDP), former king of Bhutan, King Jigme Singye Wangchuck wanted for his country to measure the quality of life in more complete terms using what he called the Gross National Happiness (GNH), striking a balance between the spiritual and material needs.

In 2013, on a planning retreat with the senior management team of the university I worked for, we were asked to develop strategies to be implemented to improve the experience of our various stakeholders. Inspired by the GNH, I proposed to develop the GIHI (Gross Institutional Happiness Index), a composite index that measures how balanced our experience is. To add a dramatic effect, I also proposed that we rename our VC (Vice Chancellor) to the CHO (Chief Happiness Officer).

GNH of Bhutan measures 9 domains and they can be adapted to education as shown in the table below. We started collecting the data to create our GIHI and interestingly, few months into the process, the Star newspaper quoted the Second Finance Minister of Malaysia, Datuk Seri Ahmad Husni Mohamad Hanadzlah, saying, "For decades, the progress of the nation has been popularly measured by the Gross Domestic Product (GDP). However, the GDP is inadequate to measure the well-being of the nation and a new approach to measure well-being effectively is required." He said this in his opening remarks before chairing the 2014 Budget Focus Group Meeting on *Developing A Malaysian Happiness Index: Work-Life Balance.*

Clearly, academic institutions have a unique opportunity to lead the society in promoting holistic human development, which seems to be a pressing need in this complex and rapidly changing world we are living in.

Domains of the Gross National Happiness Index

	GNHI	GIHI
1	Psychological well-being	Emotional well-being
2	Health	Health and Safety
3	Time use	Time use
4	Education	Learning and Staff and students Development
5	Cultural diversity and resilience	Cultural diversity and resilience
6	Good Governance	Good Governance
7	Community vitality	Community vitality
8	Ecological diversity and resilience	Campus sustainability
9	Living standards	Living standards

In February 2016, the United Arab Emirates appointed a "Minister of Happiness" to show the government's commitment to the promotion of happiness and life satisfaction amongst the residents of the state. "Happiness is a serious job for governments," said Ohood Al Roumi, the UAE's Minister of Happiness. "The main job for the government is to create happiness. In 2011, the UN encouraged the member countries to look at happiness for a holistic approach for development. The role of the government is to create an environment where people can flourish – can reach their potential – and choose to be happy." She told the CNN news channel.

The government of UAE has recently selected 60 officers from different government departments to undergo intense training in the science of happiness at leading mindfulness and positive psychology centres in the UK and USA in order to prepare them to implement the necessary policies in the happiness domain.

Not to be surpassed by Bhutan and UAE, Madhya Pradesh became the first state in India to set up a "Happiness Department" on July 2016, with chief minister Shivraj Singh Chouhan heading the department for the time being. saying it will work to ensure "happiness in the lives of common people" on the lines of Bhutan. The Happiness Department organised a happiness week where villagers in the state participated in games and other activities that are aimed at raising their levels of happiness and satisfaction.

The United Nations has adopted 20th of March as annual World Happiness Day and it now publishes an annual report entitled the World Happiness Report. The report rates the happiness levels at 157 countries. In 2016, Denmark ranked number 1 and Burundi 157 [6].

Clearly, whether at an individual, organisational or national level, happiness, emotional wellbeing and happiness are increasingly seen as serious business that needs to be approached scientifically and systematically. The coming chapters will outline certain approaches and techniques that can be utilised by individuals and organisations to develop and grow various aspects of the emotional intelligence.

EMOTIONAL INTELLIGENCE

by DANIEL GOLEMAN

	SELF	**SOCIAL-RELATIONAL**
REGULATION	**SELF MANAGEMENT** Emotional Self Control Transparency Adaptability Achievement Orientation Initiative	**RELATIONSHIP MANAGEMENT** Developing Others Inspirational Leadership Influence Change Catalyst Conflict Management Teamwork and Collaboration
AWARENESS	**SELF AWARENESS** Emotional Awareness Accurate Self Assessment Self Motivation Self Confidence	**SOCIAL AWARENESS** Empathy Organisational Awareness Service Orientation

Shoot the Boss!

(This page is intentionally left blank)

5

Self-Awareness

"And you? When will you begin that long journey into yourself?"

Rumi

"Self-awareness is our capacity to stand apart from ourselves and examine our thinking, our motives, our history, our scripts, our actions, and our habits and tendencies."

Stephen Covey

In 2010, Green Peak Partners and Cornell's School of Industrial and Labour Relations conducted a study to examine the role of business executives' interpersonal traits in the success to achieve the overall business objectives. The study examined 72 executives at public and private companies with annual revenues from $50 million to $5 billion. While the research examined a number of executive interpersonal qualities, self-awareness seems to stand out as a prognosticator of success. The search to fill leadership roles gives short shrift to self-awareness, which should actually be a top criterion. Interestingly, a high self-awareness score was the strongest predictor of overall success. This is not altogether surprising as executives who are aware of their weaknesses are often better able to hire subordinates who perform well in categories in which the leader lacks acumen. These leaders are also more able to entertain the idea that someone on their team may have an idea that is even better than their own [1].

The starting point and the cornerstone of emotional intelligence is self-awareness. It represents awareness of the stories that we tell ourselves about who we are, what is going on within us, our strengths, weaknesses and limitations. Emotionally intelligent individuals are aware of their internal state, capabilities and limitations and they are not only able to use language to describe how they feel in clear and precise words, they can select the language that can positively impact how they feel. These individuals can manage themselves better and can develop better relationships. Through awareness of what drives and motivates them, self-aware individuals are able to pursue aspirational and difficult goals, that they manage to continue to chase even if the obstacles are numerous, mainly because they have a clear sense of purpose.

According to Daniel Goleman, self-awareness encompasses emotional awareness, accurate self-assessment and self-confidence. In this chapter, we will unpack this further and provide some suggested exercises to develop self-awareness.

Emotional Awareness

Emotions are often what sets us in motion, and the basis of emotional intelligence is to be aware of our own emotions and to be able to accurately describe and express them. This is easier said than done though! One of the reasons for this is that the middle brain where emotions are processed is incapable of processing language. Try to ask people how they feel. I bet you the answer will be words like "fine", "ok" or something along these lines. Being aware of our emotional state is the first step in cultivating emotional intelligence, and developing the language to describe our emotional state is a prerequisite for achieving the emotional awareness.

To help the students who registered for my online emotional intelligence course develop the language to describe their emotions, I requested that they report their emotional and relational states daily using specific adjectives in 6 different domains, namely Mental, Emotional, Relational, Spiritual, Vocational, and Physical domains. I learned this framework from Jim Warner who coaches top executives and CEOs around the world and he starts his forum sessions with a "check in" where everyone reports her/his M.E.R.S.V.P. state. This is described in more detail in the table below.

The process of reporting one's emotions daily was difficult initially, where the students found it almost agonising as they forced themselves to describe their emotions. As time went by, the process got easier and more enjoyable. Throughout the process, I assured the students that "all emotions are OK." The purpose of the exercise was to create awareness of our feelings, and not to deny them or suppress them. Below is a sample of how course participants report their feelings daily.

My Emotions Today. Participants report how they feel daily creating more self-awareness

As you can see from the example above, often the M.E.R.S.V.P. domain reporting starts some discussions on the nature of the state of each domain. This sharpens the awareness and creates a sense of community. You can do this exercise in a number of ways. You may join the online course and perform the exercise with the other participants or you may report your daily emotions in your diary or even write them on a board at home, work or school. To help with the description of the feeling in each domain, the table below contains some suggested list of adjectives to choose from.

Sample adjectives that can be used to describe how we feel.

Domain	Definition	Sample adjectives
Mental	Mind, intellect	thinking, sharp, focused, curious, open, blocked, challenged, questioning, confused, learning, growing, wondering
Emotional	Affective state of consciousness	happy, sad, fearful, disgusted, guilty, confused, aware, excited, satisfied, loved
Relational	Quality/state of relationships	connected, grounded, networked, blessed, separated, reaching out, supported, lost, misunderstood, betrayed
Spiritual	Bigger cause/meaning	blessed, grounded, assured, doubtful, searching, enlightened, driven, betrayed, disappointed, fulfilled
Vocational	Job, career or study	progressing, stuck, challenged, stretched, supported, driven, focused, confused, realistic
Physical	Body and health	healthy, strong, in pain, flourishing, recovering, refreshed, healing, renewing

Accurate Self-Assessment

In order for us to progress in life, it is essential to be able to know our strengths, weaknesses, opportunities and threats. We also need to recognise that, at times, our strengths and weaknesses or even our opportunities and challenges are hidden in a blind spot that we are unable to see and we may need the help of others to shed some light on them. There exists a number of tools to approach accurate self-assessment. The following are two of them.

SWOT Analysis

SWOT analysis is a reflection tool to reflect on Strengths, Weaknesses, Opportunities and Threats (Challenges). Performing SWOT analysis can have a profound impact on our accurate self-assessment and self-awareness. Strengths are positive internal qualities and capabilities an individual (or an organisation) has. These can be physical traits, skills or qualities of character that can help in achieving goals. Weaknesses, on the other hand, are internal shortcomings that need to be addressed further in order to ensure the achievement of objectives. Opportunities and threats represent external events and circumstances that can potentially be useful or harmful, respectively.

	Self	Social
Benefit	Strengths	Opportunities
Harm	Weaknesses (Areas for Growth)	Threats (Challenges)

SWOT Analysis

As we perform the SWOT analysis, we can have a more accurate self-assessment, allowing us to capitalise on our strengths, use our weakness as opportunities for growth and be ready to grab opportunities, and face challenges.

Johari Window

Johari window is a self-discovery graphical tool that was created by psychologists Joseph Luft and Harrington Ingham in 1955, hence its name. It is used to help people better understand their relationship with themselves and others. It is basically a 2 by 2 matrix resulting in 4 quadrants containing what you know and do not know about yourself as well as what others know and do not know about you. This is shown in the next figure.

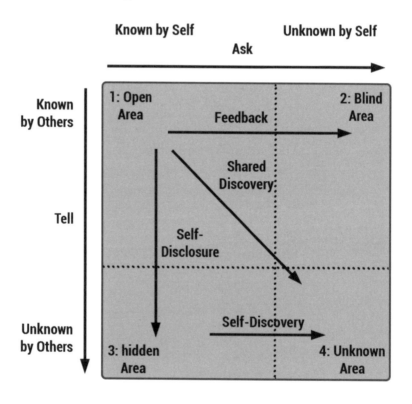

Johari Window

The four quadrants are discussed briefly below:

1. Quadrant 1 (Open Area): This contains your visible behaviour, qualifications, attitudes and values that both you and those around you recognise in you.

2. Quadrant 2 (Blind Area): These are things that others see in you that you are not aware of. Think of it as something that is smeared on your face, while you do not know of its existence, others do see it easily. This includes both physical and psychological aspects and may be either positive or negative. Examples of physical blind spots include body odour and the annoying repetitive use of some words during speech. Deeper blind spots may refer to the feelings of unworthiness and inadequacy that some of us may carry without being aware of. Positive blind spots are mainly associated with our potential. A tall person, for example, may often be seen as someone who can do well in basketball, even though that person may have not thought of playing the sport.

3. Quadrant 3 (Hidden Area): This area includes things known to you but hidden from others. This may include personal history and health related matters.

4. Quadrant 4 (Unknown Areas): Things that are unknown both to yourself and others and represent a great domain for discovery and exploration.

The Johari window can be used to achieve a number of objectives including knowing more about ourselves and bringing our team members closer to each other. In both cases, the objective is usually to widen the open area both horizontally (through asking for feedback) and vertically through revealing things to others. In the process, some discoveries in the unknown area may happen, improving self-awareness.

In a team building setup, team members may construct their own Johari windows on large flipcharts, put some descriptions in both the open area and the hidden area, then everyone sticks their window on the wall and the attendees go around and provide feedback in the blind area. It is worth mentioning here that it is important to pay attention to the social and cultural context when giving feedback and when revealing things about oneself. Some societies are more open than others when giving and receiving feedback. Trust needs to be established too to ensure that nothing that is revealed will be used against the individual who reveals it.

Self-Confidence

Armed with clear awareness of one's current state along the 6 M.E.R.S.V.P. domains and accurate self-assessment, a clear picture of an individual's potential as well as limitations emerges. This results in confidence of one's (and even organisation's) abilities to tackle challenges as they come along.

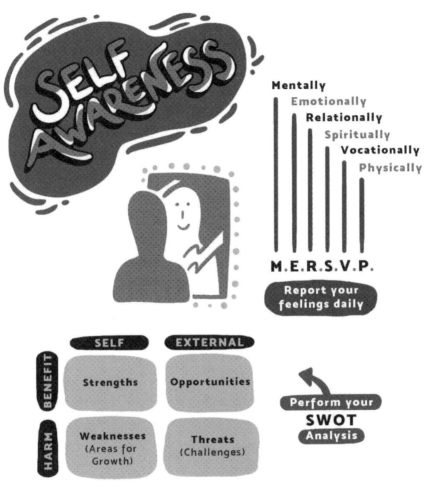

SELF AWARENESS

Mentally
Emotionally
Relationally
Spiritually
Vocationally
Physically

M.E.R.S.V.P.

Report your feelings daily

	SELF	EXTERNAL
BENEFIT	Strengths	Opportunities
HARM	Weaknesses (Areas for Growth)	Threats (Challenges)

Perform your **SWOT** Analysis

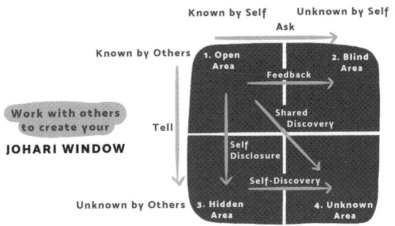

Work with others to create your **JOHARI WINDOW**

Known by Self   Unknown by Self

Ask

Known by Others

	1. Open Area	2. Blind Area
	Feedback	
	Shared Discovery	
	Self Disclosure	
	Self-Discovery	

Tell

Unknown by Others   3. Hidden Area   4. Unknown Area

Shoot the Boss!

(This page is intentionally left blank)

Chapter 6

Social-Awareness

"Opinion is really the lowest form of human knowledge. It requires no accountability, no understanding. The highest form of knowledge is empathy, for it requires us to suspend our egos and live in another's world. It requires profound purpose and larger-than-the-self kind of understanding."

Bill Bullard

"The bigger triangle is bullying the smaller one. The circle is hiding, but the bigger triangle tries to disturb it and the smaller triangle rushes to help." This is what my 10-year-old son said when I showed him a short animation that was developed by Fritz Heider depicting two triangles and a circle moving around. The bigger triangle follows the smaller one in looks like its pushing it around. My son is hardly alone in seeing drama, emotions, intentions and feelings in what should have been two triangles and a circle moving around in a two-dimensional space. As a matter of fact, almost everyone who watches the short of animation had a similar reaction. Human minds have the innate capacity to perceive others in terms of their intentional mental processes. We are always interested to know what others are thinking about and how they are thinking about it. This is called the theory of the mind and this capacity is hardwired into us and it is the basis for our social life.

Just like self-awareness, social-awareness refers to presence of the mind and other character traits that enable individuals to be aware of their surroundings and how they are impacted by and impact other people's feelings and emotions. To nurture social awareness, Daniel Goleman proposed the development of empathy, organisational awareness and service orientation.

Empathy

Empathy is the ability to put ourselves in the position of others and feel how they feel. It does not necessarily mean to agree with others, just to feel what they feel. This is extremely necessary for all social animals and it has its roots in the biology of the brain. Italian researchers discovered certain neurons in the brain that are activated not only when we go through an experience but also when we see someone going through a similar experience. That is why, for example, if we see someone accidentally hitting her finger with a hammer, we can almost feel the pain in our own fingers. These neurons are now dubbed "mirror neurons."

Empathy is a very powerful tool and those who cultivate it can be good team players. Empathy is very necessary for professional success as well. Engineers and designers, for example, need to develop empathy with the end users of their products so that they can develop human-centric designs.

Studies of the history of malpractice litigation against doctors revealed that empathetic doctors who exhibited care and listened well to their patients were at a much lower risk of being sued for malpractice by their patients when something goes wrong, compared to doctors whom were perceived as less empathetic. Empathy is also a key skill for those who work in sales, marketing and customer service.

One practical way to develop empathy in product design is to use the product through a process that is called "body storming." Imagine a group of male engineers who are designing a car that is being pitched to female customers. The body storming entails the male engineers put on high heels, carry handbags and try to get into the car and drive it. The knowledge acquired through body storming is very valuable and often ends up profoundly influencing the design process. After I turned forty, I started to have challenges in reading fine print. This includes the numbers and letters on my TV remote control as well as some name cards. Although I think that, at times, the fine print is made fine on purpose to fool consumers, in the case of my TV remote control and name cards, the designers are either young or used enlarged models of their design on their computer screens. In both cases, putting themselves in the shoes of different age groups of their end users would have significantly improved the design.

When my colleagues who are new to teaching ask me how to know if the time allocated for their final exam paper is sufficient, my advice is to choose a quiet corner and answer the exam paper as if they are sitting for it themselves and time the exercise. The time allocated for the students should be 1.5 times the time the lecturer needs to complete the paper.

To develop empathetic skills, students in my *Success with Emotional Intelligence* course on campus were grouped in pairs. Each one of the two students was asked to describe his (her) feelings while the partner listens empathetically and in a non-judgmental way. The partner then reciprocates and listens back. After that exchange, each partner narrates the feelings of his (her) partner back to him (her).

Dining in the Dark is a restaurant series that was started in 1999 to give sighted customers the experience of eating as a blind person. The restaurant is made pitch black and the food is served by blind or visually impaired individuals. The restaurant is aimed at enabling sighted people to empathise with blind people by being in their shoes for a short period of time. This also leads to more appreciation of the ability to see, an ability many of us take for granted.

In general, we can develop empathy by adopting an attitude of trying to see the world from others' point of view, actively working towards validating the opposing point of view (rather than just rejecting it outright), listening to the others' points of view and accepting to disagree.

Organisational Awareness

Organisational awareness refers to the ability to sense the dynamics of a group of people or team. This includes at which stage the team is in its growth cycle as well as the centres of power such as who calls the shots and who may be playing a negative role in the team. This awareness allows the individual to gauge the level of emotions in a group as well how can this be positively influenced.

Service Orientation

Service leadership is being recognised as a sustainable leadership style. Leadership is influence and servant leaders can command the respect of others and have a positive influence over them, enabling their teams to achieve their goals. To develop service orientation, it is important to get involved in activities that go beyond the direct benefit of an individual and have positive impact on others. Through serving others, we can develop a sense of self-worth and usefulness while building our capacity to understand the plight of those around us. Gradually, service learning is being acknowledged as a viable development technique for building emotional intelligence traits in students.

John-Son Oei is a passionate young man. After graduating with a degree in communication, he was searching for his life purpose and inner calling. "I chose to study communication because I thought it was a generic degree that will help me find what I should be doing later in life. However, after graduating I was even more confused." John-Son told my students while delivering a guest lecture as part of one of my MOOCs (Massive Open Online Courses). While enjoying life and making money modelling, John-Son felt the urge to do something more meaningful.

Travelling one day with his friends, he visited a village of one of the Malaysian indigenous people groups (called *Orang Asli* in Malay) and he was shocked to know that some of them did not have a proper home to stay in. He was particularly disturbed seeing a broken shack with a man living there. Something inside him made him feel that he should act! He set up a Facebook event inviting his friends to join him to build this man a house. He was surprised by how many people were willing to help. They spent a weekend building the house and even gave it a paint job. Encouraged by what a group of untrained but enthusiastic people can do, John-Son went on and founded EPIC (Extraordinary People Impacting Community), a social enterprise that seeks to create a cooperative world with response-able people driven by a heart of service. Through EPIC, the movement of EPIC Homes, an initiative that seeks to provide homes for the *Orang Asli* began.

EPIC Homes has a very interesting business model. It converts the home building exercise into a team building challenge that clients, such as companies and organisations can perform over a three-day period. The client will pay for the materials needed to build the house, plus the experience and EPIC Homes will supervise the client's team throughout the home building process. The home is then presented to the identified *Orang Asli* family. This service learning exercise is a very interesting and innovative initiative that EPIC Homes is pioneering. The partnership takes place between the beneficiary family and the team which is building the home. "Poverty is a state of mind," John-Son says. "In order to empower the family that will receive the home, EPIC engages village to determine the selection process and the family members in the design of their future home. They can choose a range of designs that not just fits their land practically but their personal taste too. They are also given a choice of orientation, special layout and what colour the paint will be," he added.

To ensure that the beneficiary family does not see the house as free hand-out, the family members are also required to participate in building their house and also to pay-it-forward and help build two other homes with their neighbours. This had a very interesting spill over, as members of the *Orang Asli* community participate in building their home, they develop very useful skills that have helped some of them gain employment. This has led to many empowered beneficiaries who have gone on to help other families, even outside their own village, getting involved in disaster recovery efforts outside their own state as not just builders but trainers, leaders and positive role models of service leadership to other beneficiaried. EPIC Homes has built more than 100 homes thus far, a small dent in the 12,000 homes needed by the *Orang Asli* community in Peninsular Malaysia according to John-Son.

John-Son Oei, Founder & CEO of EPIC

I had the honour to be part of the team that built a home for Juri, Masni and their three children. The project was sponsored by Taylor's University, the senior management team of the university, supervised by the EPIC Homes team, worked very hard to build a nice and simple house in three days.

The work EPIC does is an excellent example of service orientation. Service orientation is an important and necessary trait to develop social awareness through feeling the needs of others and being able to play a positive role in fulfilling these needs. We can all develop our service orientation by giving to others, helping people in our communities, volunteering and supporting worthy causes.

Building a Home for Masni and Juri (Mushtak Al-Atabi)

Develop empathy with others by

**PUTTING YOURSELF IN
THE SHOES OF OTHERS**

 Try to SEE the world from others point of view

VALIDATE the other point of view

LISTEN and accept to disagree

**BE OF SERVICE
TO OTHERS**

Volunteer

Give others

Support a worthy cause

Help people in your community

7

Self-Management

"Mastering others is strength. Mastering yourself is true power."

Lao Tzu

"The first and best victory is to conquer self."

Plato

In the 1960s, Walter Mischel and his colleagues performed a series of experiments with the pre-schoolers at Stanford University's Bing Nursery School. The test setup was straightforward, a child was asked to sit in a room and was presented with two choices; to have a tasty treat (for example, a marshmallow) right away or have two marshmallows if the child was willing and able to wait for around 20 minutes. As expected, some children were able to delay gratification and resist the temptation to enjoy the bigger reward while others did not hesitate to eat the single marshmallow. Mischel, a psychologist, was studying the dynamics of delayed gratification and self-control amongst children, however, his research resulted in some interesting insights. In a follow-up study on the same children more than a decade later, researchers found that those who were able to exert more self-control as children had better academic performance, earned more money and were even fitter than those who were unable exercise self-control. In his book *The Marshmallow Test,* Mischel examined willpower and whether it can be taught and developed. His research shows that will power can be cultivated and this is indeed great news. [1]

No matter how we define success—a happy family, robust health, fulfilling career, financial independence, self-actualisation—it seems to be associated with two personal traits, intelligence and self-management. Among these two traits, the latter is the one that we can influence and improve. Managing self is a very important component of emotional intelligence and a strong indicator of success in life. Individuals who are aware of their own emotions and their surroundings learn that all emotions are ok. It is ok to be angry, sad or happy. However, not all actions are ok, and while they cannot control what life may throw at them, they can choose the way they respond. They realise that it is not acceptable, for example, to insult others or physically harm them while we are angry or disappointed.

We will always be exposed to external events and stimuli as we go through the ups and downs of life. Angry motorists will shout at us, co-workers will misunderstand us and people will cut the queue ahead of us. We need to accept that we will never be able to control external events that happen to us. What we have control over, however, is how to respond to these events and this is called self-management. Viktor Frankl, author of *Man Search for Meaning,* said "Everything can be taken from a man but one thing: the last of human freedoms - to choose one's attitude in any given set of circumstances, to choose one's own way." An angry motorist can push our buttons, and this would surely make us angry and frustrated, but we can still choose the way to respond to this stressful situation. We can smile and even apologise to diffuse the situation or shout back and escalate the situation to a fight. [2]

To survive in the environment in which our ancestors lived, our brains evolved to quickly respond to negative stimuli and threats. If a caveman is walking in the jungle, it makes sense for him to run if he feels danger approaching rather than stopping and analysing the consequences. This fast action that served us well in the past has become a liability that we need to mitigate in today's world. There is a need to train our brains to be able to identify and quickly respond to opportunities, not only threats. This fits clearly in the realm of self-management.

The Willpower Muscle

In one of the most famous experiments in psychology, Roy Baumeister asked a group of students to fast for several hours before getting them into a room where they were allowed to eat. The aroma of freshly baked chocolate chip cookies filled the air and also the hearts of the hungry students with anticipation. As you may expect in a psychological experiment, there was a twist. The students were assigned randomly to either eat the cookies or plain raw radish. The researchers left the students alone with both the cookies and radish within their reach, simply to maximise temptation. Watching from a hidden window, the researchers observed those assigned to eat radishes wrestling with the temptation. Some took the cookies in their hands and smelled them savouring their fresh scent. To their credit, none of those assigned to the radish succumbed to the lure of eating the forbidden food. This set the stage for the final part of the experiment where all the students, including a third control group that was asked to fast but was offered no food, were told that they will be tested for cleverness using sets of puzzles. The puzzles, in fact, were unsolvable and the real aim was to see how long would the students persevere before giving up.

On average, students who ate the cookies spent 20 minutes attempting the puzzle before giving up, a similar time was scored by the control group. Interestingly the radish group gave up after only 8 minutes on average. This is considered a very significant difference.

This experiment was repeated around the world in different settings but with similar results. Willpower seems to be akin to a muscle that gets fatigued when strained. Those individuals who spent their willpower resisting the cookies had little left in their reservoir to resist giving up on the puzzles. Interestingly, just like a muscle, willpower can be trained and exercised to be stronger in order for us to have better self-control [3].

This leads to a simple and logical conclusion, one of the most effective ways to develop self-control is to avoid the depletion of the willpower reservoir through avoiding temptation. For example, if you wish to start a dieting programme, make sure that you do not have snacks that are easily accessible between meals, or even better, remove all the snacks away from your home. During the marshmallow test, children who were able to wait the whole 20 minutes avoided temptation through distracting themselves by singing, examining the furniture in the room and avoided looking at the forbidden treat.

According to Daniel Goleman, self-management entails emotional self-control, transparency, adaptability, achievement orientation, initiative and optimism. The following section describe the various techniques and activities that can be used to improve self-management. I introduced some of these techniques during my Massive Open Online Course to help cultivate different aspects of self-management. Students found these techniques and activities to be beneficial and even life changing.

Brain Rewiring

During the Korean War (1950-1953), the Chinese used what they called "lenient policy" to operate prisoner-of-war (POW) camps under their supervision. Unlike the North Korean POW camps that featured physical brutality and harsh punishment, the Chinese utilised a more psychologically focused approach to nudge captured American soldiers into submission and compliance to give military information, turn in fellow prisoners, and publicly denounce their country. The Chinese approach was so successful in getting the American POWs to collaborate with the enemy that it led to an extensive investigation by American psychologists after the war. These psychologists quizzed the returning POWs intensively to determine what had happened and how the Chinese managed to get them to inform on one another, a behaviour that was not prevalent among the American POWs in World War II.

While American servicemen were trained to provide nothing but name, rank, and serial number when captured, the Chinese captors used their keen understanding of psychology to subdue their captives. They would for example ask a POW to make simple, seemingly inconsequential, statements that were critical of the United States or were sympathetic with the communists. They will ask the POWs to agree to statements such as "the United States is not perfect," or "in communist countries, the government ensures that everyone has a job." They will then ask the POW to write these statements and sign his name to them. Slowly but surely the Chinese ensured that the Americans are committed to their "statements" by broadcasting them to the rest of the camps. Ultimately, this changes the image of a POW of himself, he now sees himself as a collaborator.

I hope that by now, this pattern is clear and recognisable to you. The Chinese were using language to alter the narratives (stories) of the POWs. The experience of American POWs during the Korean War shows us how making statements and affirming them overtime can result in changing how individuals view themselves in their own narrative leading to behaviours consistent with the new story. This realisation can be used for good too, for example, to develop a positive and optimistic view of one's self and the world. As we repeatedly mentioned, the human brain seems to be hardwired to respond to negative stimuli. This trait was very important to ensure survival in the dangerous environment that our ancestors used to inhabit.

However, this inherited asset may become a liability when it comes to situations where positive thinking and the ability to respond to opportunities are paramount. The good news is that the brain can be "rewired" to respond to positive stimuli.

One technique proposed by Tal Ben-Shahar in his book *Happiness*, to achieve this is to keep a gratitude journal reporting things that an individual is grateful for daily [4]. I have institutionalised this exercise in my *Success with Emotional Intelligence* course where all my students were required to report 5 things that they were grateful for on a daily basis for the period of 18 weeks. Just like reporting the inner state daily, the *Brain Rewiring* exercise started as being awkward and difficult, as it required different brain muscles to be trained. With time, the exercise became more fluent, easy and enjoyable. At the end of the course, students reported a more positive perspective towards life and appreciated themselves and those around them more. This positive mental attitude is extremely powerful when addressing challenges and it can cultivate the creation of innovative alternatives in both professional and personal life as well as fostering emotional self-control and optimism. Repeating this daily exercise for the period of the course was aimed at creating positive thinking attributes and literally building myelin along the mental circuits that enable us to see the goodness in situations and people. An example of *Brain Rewiring* is shown below.

Paraskevi · 2 days ago

Grateful for
Surving the day at work
Taking my daughter, for a bit, to work, which made her happy
Friends coming over tonight
The support I receive
Exercising! It really helps me tremendously to cope with stress

↳ Reply   You, Deborah Ramirez, POOJA SINGH and 1 other like this   Unlike

Deborah Ramirez ↱ Paraskevi · 2 days ago

Absolutely awesome!
You made a memory today with your daughter that she will always remember!
Good job on the exercise!
Stay awesome friend!
💝

↳ Reply   You like this   Unlike

Brain Rewiring performed daily by the course participants

Towards the end of the course, Susan, one of my online students, reported the following as one of the things that she was grateful for on January 11, 2014 "a really difficult conversation which brain rewiring enabled me to turn into a relationship building opportunity rather than a confrontation! Yeah!"

Another very interesting method to rewire the brain was reported by Mauricio Estrella. He shared this in his TED talk and a few online articles and I found it amazing. After falling in love with a beautiful young lady, then quickly getting married to her, things did not work out as planned and the marriage ended in divorce. Times were difficult to say the least and Mauricio was having difficulties to let go and move on with his life. One day, he was rushing to a meeting and needed some files from his computer, starting his computer he was confronted with a message telling him that his password has expired and he needs to set up a new one! The ICT policy of the company he worked for required that employees change their passwords monthly for security reasons. Frustrated as he was, he had a brilliant idea, "what if I use a password that will encourage me and cheer me up?"

His new password was "Forgive@h3r." "My password became the indicator. My password reminded me that I shouldn't let myself be victim of my recent break up, and that I'm strong enough to do something about it" Mauricio wrote in an article in the Huffington Post. Encouraged by how much this simple action helped him to accept what happened and move on, he went on to try new passwords to achieve different objectives. Below is a list that he shared in the same article.

Password	Impact
Forgive@her	(To Mauricio's ex-wife). It worked
Quit@smoking4ever	It worked
Save4trip@thailand	It worked
Eat2times@day	It did not work
Sleep@before12	It worked
Ask@her4date	It worked. Mauricio fell in love again
No@drinking2months	It worked
Get@c4t!	It worked. Mauricio has a beautiful cat
Facetime2mom@sunday	It worked. Mauricio talks with his mom every week

"I still await very anxiously each month so I can change my password into something that I need to get done. Remember, for added security, try to be a bit more complex with the words. Add symbols or numbers, or scramble a bit the beginning or the ending of your password string. S4f3ty_f1rst!" Mauricio added [5].

As mentioned earlier, brain activities governing behaviour, habits, learning and thought expressions occur as electric signals generated and transmitted along neurons in the brain. Neurons in the brain are widely connected and that makes the electrical signals leak as they move along this complex network of wires. Performing tasks repeatedly and intentionally, such as *Brain Rewiring*, will get the brain cells firing signals in a certain repetitive fashion. Continuous firing stimulates the formation of the electrical insulating myelin sheath that encloses the path of the electrical signal. The more the neurons fire along the same path, the thicker the myelin layer and the better the insulation. In time this will improve the strength and the speed of the electrical signals and this is how we get better at things after practicing them.

The Plexiglas Concept

The Plexiglas Concept is a simple and very useful self-management technique. It can be used in both social and professional settings. Imagine if someone is accusing you of bad things, your natural response is to feel under attack and start defending yourself, questioning the motives of the person attacking you. This often leads to escalation and usually nothing good comes out of the situation. Next time you are emotionally attacked, imagine a thick and strong sheet of Plexiglas standing between you and the attacker and imagine what you are attacked with is a physical object, a rotten fruit for example. Now as the attacker throws the object (insult, accusation) at you, you could see him or her and as the thrown object hits the Plexiglas it splatters allowing you to see its content.

From your safety behind your Plexiglas, you look at the attacker and the object and say to yourself, curiously, "how interesting!" This will allow you time to think and retell the story of what has just happened before responding. As the attacking projectile thrown at you gets smashed, metaphorically, on your trusted Plexiglas, you will get to examine its contents closely allowing you the opportunity to further understand the attack and the attacker. There will definitely be some negative content such as envy, hatred and misunderstanding, but there will be some useful feedback as well. Best of all, once you used the Plexiglas to allow you to delay your response, you can use the time to select the response that you prefer for that situation.

Purpose, Vision and Mission

A strong, and if done right; effective, story editing tool is having a well-defined and compelling purpose, vision and mission statement. They help motivate us and draw our attention to the bigger picture and encourage others to support us and join our cause. These days most organisations have these statements crafted and displayed on their walls. When done meaningfully and correctly, the vision and mission can provide a powerful tool to outline and communicate the purpose and core values of an organisation, or an individual. A mission statement provides the description of the purpose or "why" the individual (or organisation) exists.

Daniel Pink, the author of *Drive: The surprising truth about what motivates us*, outlines that ultimately what motivates us is the pursuit of mastery, autonomy and purpose. Mastery refers to that urge in us to get better at what matters to us which leads to acquiring better skills. Autonomy is about having a choice to be self-directed. Purpose is the desire to work on something meaningful that goes beyond one's self. In order for us, individuals and organisations alike, to explore what our purpose is and how it sits together with other important things in life, I found the Venn diagram below useful. It shows purpose at the intersection of doing what you love, what you are great at, what the world needs and what will you be paid for [6].

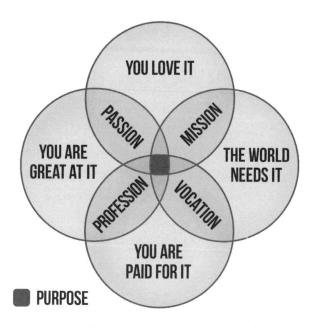

Identifying Your Purpose

Individuals can have more than one mission, for example, a professional and personal mission, these will describe the professional purpose and the family purpose of the person respectively. Missions can be outward or inward looking. Usually an inward-looking mission focuses on personal benefits and it is difficult to inspire others to join and support; an example of an inward mission "to be a millionaire by the age of 25." Outward looking missions usually have impacts beyond the individual and they can resonate with others who may support and help. An example of an outward looking professional mission for a teacher is "to help all my students realise and unleash their full potential."

A vision is a statement of what an individual (or organisation) wants the world (or themselves) to be when the mission is achieved. For example, when the individual with the mission to be a millionaire achieves his (her) mission, he (she) can have "total financial freedom" and this could be his (her) vision. For the teacher who wants to unleash the students' potential, a vision may be "a world with no illiteracy" or "a highly competitive nation."

S.M.A.R.T. Goals

In order for a person or an organisation to achieve their mission and vision, planning and goal setting is a key activity. While mission and vision may take a lifetime to achieve, goals need to be set and achieved in a more foreseeable timescale. In order to ensure the achievement of goals that accumulate towards mission achievement, goals need to be Specific, Measurable, Attainable, Relevant, and Time-bound. Below is a quick review of each aspect of the S.M.A.R.T. goals:

Specific Goals

A specific goal is clear and not ambiguous. It needs to indicate who is involved in achieving it, what needs to be accomplished, where will it take place, when will it happen and how will it be achieved. For example, "to get in shape" is rather a general goal while "join a gym and work out 3 times a week for a minimum of 1 hour at a time" is a specific goal.

Measurable Goals

Here we need to specify the metrics for measuring the goal so that we can clearly know when the goal is achieved. For example, "increase sales" is not measurable while "increase sales by 10% compared to last year" is measurable.

Attainable Goals

For goals to be attainable there should be no ethical or legal barrier against them. When setting goals, one also needs to acknowledge the environmental and physical limitations. For goals to motivate, they need to represent a stretch on what is perceived as being possible while simultaneously ensuring that the skills, capabilities and attitudes that make the goals attainable are within the reach of those who are working on them. For example, if I do not know how to swim now, setting a goal of winning an Olympic medal in 6 months is not realistic and may demotivate me as I go about my weekly training. However, the goal of qualifying for a local swimming competition within a year, is a very motivating goal; even though it stretches me, if I train long enough, I have a very good shot at achieving it.

Relevant Goals

The goals we set ought to be relevant and congruent with the overall mission and objectives of the team or the organisation. A football coach, for example, may set the goal of "making 2 egg sandwiches by 9 am". The goal is specific, measurable, attainable and time-bound but it is hardly relevant if the overall objective is to increase the tactical skills of the team. Relevant goals are worthwhile, they add real value and capitalise on the strengths and capabilities of the team members.

Time-Bound Goals

The goals need to have clear timelines indicating when they will be achieved.

While setting S.M.A.R.T. goals is a very important activity, it is essential here to remain flexible, agile and open to review the goals should an interesting unforeseen opportunity arises. If we work in the mining business and while digging for silver, we find gold, we should have the mental agility to change our goals to capture the new "golden" opportunity.

When I worked on my PhD research, my project focused on exploring the relationship between fluid mechanics and the formation of gallstones in the gallbladder. The work involved building models of the cystic ducts of patients who underwent surgical removal of the gallbladder and studying the flow inside them. While observing the flow structures I noticed that there was some fluid mixing occurring within the cystic duct that connects the gallbladder to the rest of the biliary system. While, strictly speaking, my S.M.A.R.T. goal was to explore the relationship between gallstones and the mechanics of the flow, I opted to pursue the mixing opportunity as a viable industrial option. This ended up being a significant part of my doctorate work and even influenced the title of my thesis which I changed to be *Cystic Duct to Static Mixer: A Serendipitous Journey*.

Let me iterate again, setting S.M.A.R.T. goals are very important for successful planning. However, maintaining an open mind and preserving intellectual agility allows us to adjust the S.M.A.R.T. goals to yield the best outcome should there be a change that was not foreseen when the goal was set.

Smile and the World Will Smile with You

When you're smilin'....keep on smilin'

The whole world smiles with you

And when you're laughin'....keep on laughin'

The sun comes shinin' through

But when you're cryin'.... you bring on the rain

So stop your frownin'....be happy again

Cause when you're smilin'....keep on smilin'

The whole world smiles with you"

The above are the lyrics of one of Louis Armstrong's songs [7] which may prove to be true in more ways than one. While the common perception is that emotions precede facial expression, we feel happy and then we smile, or we feel sad and then we frown; scientific evidence is now pointing towards a more complex feedback loop between facial expressions and emotions. When you smile, you can start a chain reaction that will end up with you feeling better and happier, and by the same token, frowning can make you feel sad.

Paul Ekman, one of the leading authorities on emotions and facial expressions, was performing experiments with his colleagues on their own faces to identify the facial muscles associated with different emotions. They used electrodes to stimulate these muscles and individually activate them. When they stimulated the muscles controlling frowns, they were surprised that they felt rather miserable at the end of the working day. This led them to the hypothesis that activating certain muscles through smiling and frowning can generate the corresponding emotions [8]. This has since been confirmed by a number of experiments.

Recently, research performed by psychologists at the University of Cardiff in Wales suggested that individuals who received Botox facial treatment which inhibited the muscles associated with frowning, making it difficult to frown; reported being happier and less anxious on average compared to a control group that did not receive Botox treatment. The researchers corrected for the feeling of attractiveness among the studied individuals to ensure that the emotional improvement is not related to the psychological boost associated with the cosmetic treatment [9].

We still do not fully understand the mechanisms with which our facial expressions affect our emotions and moods. However, what is sure is that when we smile we can impact our mood positively and the opposite is correct when we frown. So "keep on smilin."

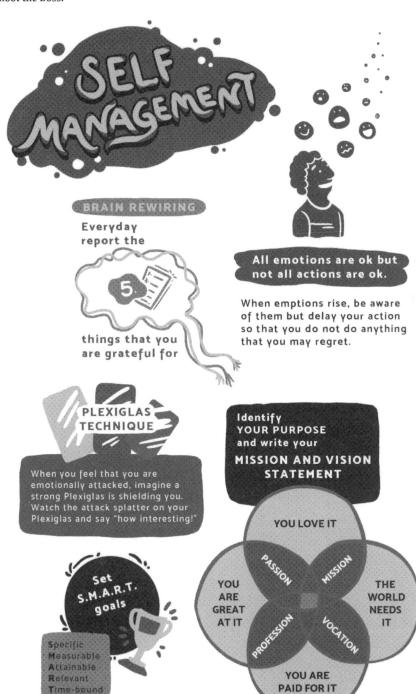

SELF MANAGEMENT

BRAIN REWIRING

Everyday report the **5** things that you are grateful for

All emotions are ok but not all actions are ok.

When emptions rise, be aware of them but delay your action so that you do not do anything that you may regret.

PLEXIGLAS TECHNIQUE

When you feel that you are emotionally attacked, imagine a strong Plexiglas is shielding you. Watch the attack splatter on your Plexiglas and say "how interesting!"

Identify **YOUR PURPOSE** and write your **MISSION AND VISION STATEMENT**

Set **S.M.A.R.T. goals**

Specific
Measurable
Attainable
Relevant
Time-bound

YOU LOVE IT

PASSION

MISSION

YOU ARE GREAT AT IT

THE WORLD NEEDS IT

PROFESSION

VOCATION

YOU ARE PAID FOR IT

Chapter 8
Relationship Management

"Relationships are all there is. Everything in the universe only exists because it is in relationship to everything else. Nothing exists in isolation. We have to stop pretending we are individuals that can go it alone."

Margaret Wheatley

"What keeps us happy and healthy as we go through life?" with this question, the psychiatrist Robert Waldinger started his TED talk in November 2015. In a recent survey of millennials that Wadlinger cited, over 80% of the respondents said that getting rich was their major life goal. Another 50% of these same young adults said that another major life goal was to become famous. Robert Waldinger is not an ordinary man, he is the director of 75-year-old Harvard study on adult development, which is one of the most comprehensive longitudinal studies in history. The study was commissioned in 1938 with 724 men both from Harvard College and Boston's poorest neighbourhoods. Participants in the study are contacted annually and asked questions about their work, home life and health. When Waldinger delivered his TED talk, 60 of the initial participants were still participating in the study [1].

The finding of the study was simple "good relationships keep us happier and healthier." This sounds simple enough, and at a certain level it feels expected, so how on earth so many people are thinking of money and fame as their major goals in life? Shouldn't we all spend more time and effort on cultivating great relationships with our loved ones and with our communities at large? What leadership failure resulted in this situation? And more importantly, what kind of social, educational and political leadership is necessary to enable individuals and communities to achieve their potential and live successful, balanced and happy lives?

The research done in the areas of human happiness, motivation and success in the past two decades is pointing in the direction of emotional intelligence and nurturing successful relationships as the bedrock for how individuals and communities remain motivated, resilient, happy and connected.

The question of happiness and how to achieve it is one of the essential questions that humanity spent centuries trying to find an answer for. Often what we think will make us happy, loses its appeal soon after we achieve it or possess it. Understanding what keeps us happy, healthy, motivated and satisfied in today's world is a pressing need as we live in a highly complex and interconnected world where the stakes are very high. This has great implications for education and family life as well as the business world.

While self-awareness is the cornerstone of the emotional intelligence, relationship management is its ultimate objective. As mentioned earlier, happiness is measured by the quality of relationships that we cultivate with those around us. The pillars of the character of an individual who is capable of nurturing and managing great relationships with others include being able to develop others, inspirational leadership, influence, being a change catalyst, conflict management as well as teamwork and collaboration. These traits are discussed below.

Developing Others

A distinct sign of emotionally intelligent individuals and leaders is a genuine interest in developing others. An exercise we did to inculcate the skill of developing others in the students who took my *Success with Emotional Intelligence* course on campus was to pair students together, and get them to interview each other to document each other's mission, vision, SWOT analysis and a SMART goal to be achieved by the end of the semester. Each student was encouraged to conduct the interview with care and respect and carefully write down the mission, vision, SWOT and the SMART goal of his (her) partner.

At the end of the exercise, each student would have to face his (her) partner and say their name followed by "your SMART goal is _____ and I know that you will achieve it." Students are also asked to send each other specific encouraging messages related to their SMART goals twice a week. This can be done verbally, using email, text messages or even with a card. After completing the exercise, one of my students posted the following on the course website:

"Today I would like to share something that I should've shared a few weeks back. So during one of the lectures, we conducted an activity called mission partnership. I was hoping to be paired up with my best friend. But eventually I was paired up with another person. A boy from Kazakhstan named Ben (not his real name) At first I was dreading it and thought that I was going to fail the activity due to his lack of English communication skills and his 'blur'ness. But after starting the activity, my eyes were opened. I could see from his perspective, I was able to see what I could do. I was able to see the difficulties he was facing. And it broke my heart. Judging before doing. And I would just like to thank Mr. Mushtak for that class and the activity and like to say sorry to Ben. This activity has opened my eyes. And I urge my fellow colleagues, don't judge and get into the person's shoes."

Another powerful way to build relationships is through gratitude. Showing gratitude develops both those who receive it and those who deliver it. It also develops and touches others through providing a positive example. One memorable and impactful way to show gratitude is the "Gratitude Visit" described by Martin Seligman, the bestselling author and one of the leading researchers in positive psychology. Seligman used this technique in a positive psychology study in 2005, where the exercise resulted in measurable positive psychological impact on those involved. To perform the exercise, you need to identify a person who had a positive impact on you and write him or her a thank you letter. The letter is ideally no more than one page long and it is written using very specific language showing why are you grateful and for what. Think of the specific thoughts and emotions that were associated with the impact that you are grateful for and record that. The letter can be structured in three parts as follows:

1. Identify the benefit: For example, "Thank you for preparing the financial reports for me to use in my meeting, even before I ask you to do so."

2. Recognise the effort: For example, "You did that despite your very busy schedule and having many deadlines to meet."

3. Praise the strength: For example, "This speaks volume to how a great team player you are. You always put the interest of the team head. We are truly blessed to have you around."

Once the letter is written, you will need to make an appointment to see the person to whom the letter is intended for without telling them about the letter. Make it a surprise! When you see the person, read the letter out loud to him or her. You may want to laminate or even frame the letter and present it as a gift that the recipient can hang it on the wall or keep it at their desks [2].

You may want to make gratitude to be a hallmark of your lifestyle and do these gratitude visits frequently to different individuals who have impacted you. To start a domino effect, you may want to suggest to the recipient of the letter that she/he send a thank you letter to a deserving individual.

Inspirational Leadership

Leadership is a human quality that is both important and difficult to define at the same time. I would like to define leadership as the ability and willingness to exhibit initiative in face of uncertainty and take responsibility for the results. Leadership also entails having a vision for a better future and readiness to serve others. It is important to remember that leadership is seldom about the position. Anyone who has a vision for doing things better, to serve others and improve their life and who takes initiative to bring along the positive change while taking responsibility for her (his) action can be described as a leader. I see this definition of leadership as liberating as it implies that anyone of us can practice leadership without waiting to be officially appointed.

For those who hold an official position of leadership, the expectations are clear. They need to serve, show the way and be ready to take responsibility and face the consequences of their actions and decisions. They need to be ready to take blame for failure and share credit for success.

Influence and Change

Emotionally intelligent individuals can positively influence those around them and be agents of constructive change in their environments. One such individual is Jack Sim, the founder of WTO (World Toilet Organisation). At the age of 40 and after staring 16 successful businesses, Jack Sim had what he called a mid-life crisis when he started to question his own purpose. Realising that millions of people around the world do not have access to proper toilets, Jack decided to do something about it. "I was an academic failure as I had

111

no degree. I also had no status and no authority," Jack said. "Starting on a shoe-string budget and the hope to change the world, I had no choice but to attempt to enact change through influencing others to act," he added. Jack calls his framework of change and influence O.P. (Other People). The idea is very simple, if you are clever enough and have a worthy cause, you can leverage unlimited resources to your cause; these include Other People's money, talent, authority, time, power and brand.

Realising that there were a number of Toilet Organisations around the world, Jack founded the World Toilet Organisation in Singapore in 2001. He managed to convince various organisations that it is a good idea to have their HQ in Singapore. From the start, Jack used humour to break the taboo associated with toilets. This started with him playing on the WTO acronym, which belongs to the World Trade Organisation, this did not only end with him getting photographed wrapped with toilet paper and carrying a plunger, leveraging media, business leaders, politicians and even Hollywood and Bollywood superstars to the cause, Jack was able to help many communities around the world, especially in India and Africa. In 2010, the World Toilet Organisation established the SaniShop which managed to sell 5,000 toilets thus far. The business model of the SaniShop is based on enabling communities to build their own toilets and improve sanitation and health in the process.

Seeing that female toilets in public places often have a long que, compared to male toilets, Jack lobbied the Singaporean authorities to change the building code increasing the ratio of female toilets to male toilets from 1:1 to 5:3 in public areas with heavy usage, such as shopping malls, cinemas, convention halls and MRT stations. For every three male cubicles or urinals, there will be five cubicles for females.

Jack continues to influence people (Other People, O.P. as he calls them) to act. His latest O.P. leverage is the production of a full-length feature comedy film "Everybody's Business." The story of this Lee Thean Jeen movie revolves around 50 Singaporeans getting food poisoning because of toilet hygiene issues. The fictional Minister of Toilets, together with hygiene officers of the Ministry of Toilets, go around trying to reach the bottom of the matter. Once again, Jack manages to use humour to break the taboo and delivers the message.

When Jack spoke to my students his advice was very simple, if you know what your purpose is and believe in making a difference, then think of the abundance in the world around you. If you align "Other People" to your goals, the cause will always be the winner.

The United Nations recognised has Jack Sim's efforts and World Toilet day is currently celebrated on the 19th of November.

Jack Sim. Founder of World Toilet Organisation.

Managing Conflicts

As more and more human activities involve working with people from different backgrounds, cultures and nationalities, conflict may be inevitable and it can range from argument, disagreement, and emotional tension to fighting or war. The conflict often starts with a misunderstanding or disagreement, if parties agree to disagree, there will be no conflict. In the book *Hostage at the Table* by George Kohlieser, the following sources for conflict are identified:

1. Differences in Goals
2. Differences in Interests
3. Differences in Values
4. Differences in Communication styles
5. Differences in Power and Status
6. Insecurity
7. Resistance to Change
8. Role Confusion
9. Search for Ego Identity
10. Personal Needs
11. Poor Communication

To effectively manage conflicts, a bond between the conflicting parties needs to be maintained at all times. Couples with different religion, racial or political orientations can keep the bond and manage any conflicts that they may have. The misunderstanding that causes disagreement and conflict can stem from misunderstanding of one's self and misunderstanding of others. If we do not know what we want or what others want, or if we do not know how we feel or how others feel, misunderstanding can happen and it can lead to conflict [3]. By now you can imagine that self-awareness is the antidote to misunderstanding of self, and social awareness is the antidote for misunderstanding others.

Practically, you can use the approach below to resolve conflict as described in *Resolving Conflict Creatively* by Linda Lantieri [4]:

1. Calm down, tune into your feelings, and express them.
2. Show a willingness to work things out by talking over the issue rather than escalating it with more aggression.
3. Try to find equitable ways to resolve the dispute, working together to find a resolution that both sides can embrace

Issues Clearance

A structured way to resolve conflicts is called "issues clearance." It is a powerful way of resolving conflicts through acknowledging the role of stories and emotions in them. This requires training, discipline and commitment. Both parties taking part in the issues clearance process should be familiar with it for the best results. That is why it works better in teams and organisation where the members are familiar with both the process and the language of this technique. The process goes like this:

1. The individual having issues, A, approaches the person with whom they have issues with, B, and says "I have something important to talk to you about, is this a good time?" You can also use an equivalent variation such as "I have an issue that I wish to clear with you, is this a good time?"
2. Once the time to discuss the issue is agreed upon, individual A then states the facts of the matter by saying "the facts are........." this is done by sticking to facts and avoiding any judgements.
3. Individual A says "The story I told myself is ...." Here the individual can narrate her/his judgement of the matter and can use expressions like, "in my opinion....," "my judgement was...."
4. Then individual A then acknowledges his/her emotions by saying "I feel ...." and then the emotions associated with the issues are expressed. These may include sad, lonely, disrespected, afraid, confused, etc.
5. Individual A owns his/her role in the issue by saying "my role in this is...." This is a very important stage that gets the person to reflect over his/her role in creating or sustaining the situation.

6. Individual A specifically states what he/she wants by saying "And I specifically want......."

7. Now individual B reflects back by repeating the whole thing he/she has just heard, facts, story, the emotions associated, the role, and the wants. This is done without interpretation and with the spirit of trying to understand. The reflection is followed by a question by the reflector "is this accurate?" Reflection should be repeated until individual A is satisfied with its accuracy. This is very necessary so that individual A feels listened to.

8. After the reflection is complete, individual B asks "is there more?" This is asked in a genuine and curious manner.

Going through this process enables both parties to empathise with each other and examine their emotions and their role in creating and prolonging the conflict. This can promote mutual understanding and conflict resolution.

The following is a real example of using the Issues Clearance process; Tania (not her real name) was selected by the CEO of the organisation to be part of a strategic transformation team. Before launching the project, another team member called for a meeting for the team with the CEO to discuss the project scope and success measures. The other two team members and the CEO responded to the meeting invitation by accepting it. Tania was silent and did not respond to the meeting invitation. The other two members felt that Tania might not be a suitable member of the team and wanted to discuss this with the CEO. On the morning when the meeting was supposed to take place, the project leader asked to meet the CEO together with team members, apart from Tania, who came to the meeting despite that fact that she did not send a response to the meeting organiser. The team wanted to share with the CEO that they had some concerns related to Tania's style of work.

When Tania was asked to excuse herself while the rest of the team had a pre-meeting discussion with CEO, she was clearly unhappy as she left the room. The CEO promised the team members that he will make sure that Tania will be more sensitive and responsive to the team's needs including accepting meeting invitations. After the meeting, Tania went to see the CEO personally to record that she was unhappy with the way she was treated. The CEO suggested that Tania clear the issues with the team. The process went like this.

"Today I went to the project meeting that you called for and I was asked to leave the room" Tania started by stating the facts of the matter.

"The story that I told myself was that the other team members did not want me to be in the team. In my opinion, the other team members are close friends and they prefer to work without me," she continued by stating the story she told herself. "This made me feel rejected, sad and threatened," Tania added acknowledging her emotions. "My role in this situation is that I did not communicate with the team members and I did not respond to the meeting invite. I also assumed that the fact I was asked to excuse myself from the meeting was a threat to me," Tania continued as she acknowledged her role in the issue she is clearing. Finally, she stated that what she wanted is "to be respected and appreciated."

The team leader reflected back to Tania what she just narrated by saying "I hear you say that you were asked to leave the meeting this morning. The story you told yourself is that the other team members did not want you to be in the team and that made you feel sad, threatened and rejected. You acknowledged your role in creating the situation by the lack of communication on your part and by assuming that having the morning meeting without you as a threat. What you want for yourself is to be respected and appreciated. Is that accurate?" "Yes" Tania replied. The team leader followed by saying "is there more?" to which she replied "no."

The team leader was able to reflect to Tania what she said because he listened carefully and kept an open mind. I witnessed situations where the reflecting was repeated more than 5 times before it receives the acceptance of the person clearing the issue.

It is useful to say here that the purpose of this process is not to get each party what they wanted but rather to get them to hear each other and put the conflict on the path of resolution. This process of issue clearance will work when you have both parties willing to play by the roles and are trained in the process.

For this specific example, the conflict was eventually resolved and everyone on the team ended up appreciating the special skills each team member brings to the table.

Teamwork and Collaboration

Teamwork is a necessary collaborative skill; it is very difficult to imagine success without it. The challenges that are presented by today's complex environment can only be addressed by highly effective teams of people from different walks of life. Although teamwork is one of the highly sought-after skills, employers around the world are complaining that academic programmes are unable to equip the graduates with the necessary skills to work well in teams. This section attempts to provide a simple and clear methodology to develop skills and techniques that can go a long way in ensuring sustainable team success.

Team Evolution

Teamwork is a complex human interaction that requires certain skills that can be learned and developed over time. This starts with understanding the various stages a group of people who are working together as a team normally go through. The Tuckman Model is one of the best models that describes how a team evolves and can provide a useful insight into human interaction in a team.

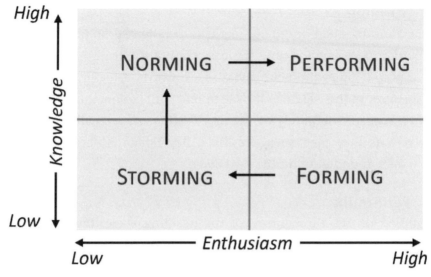

Tuckman Model

1. Forming

Forming is the first stage of team evolution. The team members are normally selected because of their capabilities and skills related to the project. During this stage, the enthusiasm among the team members is high, but the knowledge of the tasks assigned to them and their teammates, as well as the team dynamics, is usually low.

2. Storming

As time goes by and tasks accumulate, enthusiasm wears off but knowledge may not necessarily grow. The combination of low enthusiasm and low knowledge leads to stress and conflict, and different team members respond differently; some will be disappointed and confused, whereas some will just withdraw. The storming stage is a difficult one but it is necessary in order to move into the remaining team evolution stages. The key is to be able to recognise the storming stage when it happens and go through it swiftly.

3. Norming

The norming stage is where leadership potential shines. Normally what happens is that some (at least one) of the team members take charge and pulls the team members towards achieving the team's objectives. In this stage, enthusiasm may still be low, but knowledge and respect are definitely on the rise. Team members will start to taste success as they meet task deadlines. This stage is necessary to lay down the foundation for the next stage.

4. Performing

Building on the momentum of the norming stage, the performing stage features high knowledge and high enthusiasm. Arriving at this stage is a hallmark of successful teamwork. In this stage, respect and appreciation for team members' individual qualities are prevalent. Team members also have an accurate self-assessment of their own strengths and capabilities.

Team Building Exercises

After selecting the team members, we can accelerate and boost the team performance through a variety of team building exercises. These are activities that the team members can do together. Normally, team members will do some fun exercises as a group. These can include solving some interesting mental or physical challenges or even cooking. Through these exercises, team members get to appreciate each other and the diversity that they bring to the team. Team building can be done with newly formed teams or pre-existing teams that are given new tasks or wish to rekindle the team spirit.

It is also useful for teams to agree on the rules of their interactions and engagements and write down these rules and even display them, as a reminder, in the place where the group often meets. Jim Warner, in his book *Aspirations of Greatness*, gives an excellent example for such rules represented by the 13 principles below [5].

1. I will respect confidentiality
2. I will be present in the moment
3. I will stay around when times get tough
4. I will be on time and stay until the end
5. I will speak my truth
6. I will ask for what I want
7. I will take care of myself
8. I will listen with curiosity and openness
9. I will own my judgements
10. I will own my feelings
11. I will not blame, shame or fix others
12. I will ask permission before offering feedback
13. I forgive myself and others for mistakes

The above 13 principles are particularly useful to create a safe environment to tackle difficult issues and progress the team when things are tough towards the performing stage.

Our happiness is ultimately measured by

THE QUALITY of the relationships we have with our loved ones and those around us.

Have a MISSION PARTNER so that you support each others as you go about actualising your Mission.

Perform a GRATITUDE VISIT

Write a Thank You Letter that has these 3 parts

- Identify the Benefit
- Recognise the Effort
- Praise the Strength

Visit the intended person
Read the letter out loud to her/him

Have a TEAM CHARTER

List the rules of engagement that govern how the team members should communicate and interact with each other. The team charter should be agreed upon by the team members and preferably displayed for the members to be able to refer to easily.

Use "ISSUE CLEARANCE" to resolve conflict

HIGH

Knowledge

NORMING → PERFORMING

STORMING ← FORMING

LOW

LOW   Enthusiasm   HIGH

Work with others IN TEAMS

and be aware of the team development stages.

9

Telling the Story

"A man's character may be learned from the adjectives which he habitually uses in conversation."

Mark Twain

I hope that by now we have established the importance of the stories we tell in our heads in shaping our lives and the lives of those around us. Our ability to communicate, educate, motivate and lead change depends on our ability to encourage others to change their stories and building environments in which better stories thrive. One of the best ways to communicate and inspire is through telling great stories. In this chapter, we will explore communication strategies that we can use to tell amazing stories and communicate effectively.

Communication Strategies

Every day, from the moment we wake up to the moment we go to sleep, we are continuously communicating. Even if we do not notice, the advertisement on billboards as we go to work or school and the websites that we visit are always trying to communicate their messages to us. Companies want us to buy their products and they try to communicate why we need these products and how they are superior to others. We communicate with our team members, friends, parents, and children seeking their cooperation and understanding. One way or another, the purpose of communication is to communicate messages and change behaviour. Salespeople want to communicate how superior their products are (message) and want their customers to buy those products (behaviour); teachers want to communicate knowledge (message) and want their students to learn (behaviour); and politicians want to communicate their political views and policies (message) and want the citizens to vote for them (behaviour). In this context, it is fair to say that successful communication is when the right message is communicated to the right audience and it stays in their mind to create the desired behaviour. To be consistent with the message of this book, we can also say often the objective of communication is to redirect the stories audience tell in their heads, and what a better way to change someone's story that with another story.

In his book, *TED Talks: The Official TED Guide to Public Speaking*, Chris Anderson gave two examples of how to tell and how not to tell a story. The two examples describe the same situation. Here is how the story should be told. "Once, when I was eight years old, my father took me fishing. We were in a tiny boat, five miles from shore, when a massive storm blew in. Dad put a life jacket on me and whispered in my ear, "Do you trust me, son?" I nodded. He threw me overboard. I kid you not. Just tossed me over! I hit the water and bobbed up to the surface, gasping for breath. It was shockingly cold. The waves were terrifying. Monstrous. Then dad dived in after me. We watched in horror as our little boat flipped and sank. But he was holding me the whole time, telling me it was going to be OK. Fifteen minutes later, the Coast Guard helicopter arrived. It turned out that Dad knew the boat was damaged and was going to sink, and he had called them with our exact location. He guessed it was better to chuck me in the open sea than risk getting trapped when the boat flipped. And that is how I learned the true meaning of the word trust."

Here's how not to tell the same story. "I learned trust from my father when I was eight years old and we got caught in a storm while out fishing for mackerel. We failed to catch a single one before the storm hit. Dad knew the boat was going to sink, because it was one of those Saturn brand inflatable boats, which are usually pretty strong, but this one had been punctured once and Dad thought it might happen again. In any case, the storm was too big for an inflatable boat and it was already leaking. So he called the Coast Guard rescue service, who, back then, were available 24/7, unlike today. He told them our location, and then, to avoid the risk of getting trapped underwater, he put a life jacket on me and threw me overboard before jumping in himself. We then waited for the Coast Guard to come and, sure enough, 15 minutes later the helicopter showed up—I think it was a Sikorsky MH-60 Jayhawk—and we were fine."

Chris Anderson goes on saying "The first story has a character you care about and intense drama that builds to incredulity before being beautifully resolved. The second version is a mess. The drama is killed by revealing the father's intent too early; there's no attempt to share the actual experience of the kid; there are too many details included that are irrelevant to most of the audience, while other germane details like the giant waves are ignored. Worst of all, the key line that anchors the story, "Do you trust me, son?", is lost. If you're going to tell a story, make sure you know why you're telling it, and try to edit out all the details that are not needed to make your point, while still leaving enough in for people to vividly imagine what happened." [1]

Communication can be verbal or non-verbal. In the book titled *The Tipping Point*, Malcolm Gladwell explored a number of ideas that "stuck" and became phenomena that were talked about, shared, and eventually changed history [2]. Inspired by Gladwell's book, Chip and Dan Heath wrote their book *Made to Stick* and identified the features that an idea, a story or a communicated message can aspire to have in order for it to stick and result in a change of behaviour of the receiver. *Made to Stick* utilises a framework that uses the acronym SUCCES, which stands for Simple, Unexpected, Concrete, Credible, Emotional and Stories [3]. I added another S, "Show not only tell." The message or story need not have all the 7 elements of the SUCCESS framework, but having 3 or more of these elements improves its chances at being remembered and having an impact. I shall describe each part of the SUCCESS framework in the sections below.

Simple

This is one of the most important components of the SUCCESS framework and we should always strive to incorporate it in our storytelling and communication strategies. People will always remember simple stories and messages better than complex ones. The interesting thing is that, often simple is more difficult to achieve than complex. To simplify anything, one must be very well versed with all of its aspects. Apple products, for example, are known to be simple and easy to use; this simplicity is the outcome of the labour of many designers and engineers who worked tirelessly to fully comprehend how the products are to be used, and designed them for a memorable user experience. In short, simple is not easy. One of Picasso's paintings, the Bull, illustrates this concept well. Picasso drew 11 paintings of a bull starting with a life-like drawing of the bull and progressively removing parts of it in a quest to reach the essence of the bull. The eleventh painting uses only few lines to represent the bull. It is simple but Picasso reached this simplicity through his mastery of the complex.

If you have an idea, a message or a concept that you wish to communicate, you will need first to really comprehend its essence. This essence can be the basis of your communication strategy. You will need to be able to explain your concept with as few words as possible, stripping any part that is not core for the message. Simple messages are compact and profound while conveying the core essence of what needs to be communicated. Just like in the story narrated above by

Chris Anderson, he intentionally opted to remove a number of details while maintaining the essence which is learning about trust.

Picasso's "The Bull". (Source: takeovertime.co)

Using metaphors is another way of simplifying communication. The word metaphor is from the Greek word "metaphora" which means to transfer. So, a metaphor is a mental shortcut in which we can use a familiar concept to communicate a less familiar one, by transferring our understanding of the existing concept to the new one. When DNA was introduced as an evidence in criminal justice, lawyers and judges struggled with understanding and accepting it. One way to communicate how DNA can help in delivering justice was the metaphor introducing DNA as the new fingerprint.

Unexpected

"Bill Gates just released mosquitoes into the audience at TED and said, 'Not only poor people should experience this.'" This was a tweet by Dave Morin who witnessed Bill Gates releasing mosquitoes into the hall during his TED talk about malaria. The mosquitoes did not carry malaria, nonetheless having them released into the audience is probably the last thing you would expect during a talk about malaria. This act has, for sure, grabbed the attention of many and went viral on nd memorable [4].

We have explored the role the old brain plays in responding to what is perceived as a threat. This part of the brain is wired to make us react quickly to situations that are out of the ordinary, and it is responsible for the fight or flight reaction. That is why shocking, surprising, and unexpected events or information seize our attention more than expected ones. If you go for a lecture on your first day of university and your Thermodynamics lecturer arrives in blue suit and a black tie, this will not be remarkable, but if he instead arrives in a clown outfit, I bet you will never forget this event even after a long time! Always look for an unexpected angle to pitch or deliver your message. The unexpectedness can be achieved through how the message is crafted, the medium used to deliver it, or who delivers it.

Blendtec is a company that makes blenders, and in order to advertise how strong their blenders are, they made a series of videos showing their blenders in action. They did not demonstrate their blenders mixing fruits and vegetables; instead they did something highly unexpected. They filmed their blenders mixing everything from golf balls to iPhones. These videos are in a series of videos called *Will it blend?*. I watched the "blending" of an iPhone 5S and 4 iPhone 5Cs (the full colour range) and the blender turned them into dust! This video has over 2 million views on YouTube. *Will it Blend?* videos are also available at *http://www.willitblend.com*. This sure had an impact on me as I am planning to buy one of these blenders.

When my school wanted to put a newspaper advertisement to promote engineering as a career option, we looked for an unexpected angle to pitch that. While a typical advertisement promoting engineering may talk about the role of engineers in building different technological gadgets, we used the fact that 33% of CEOs of the world's top 500 companies have an engineering degree as the main point of the ad. According to The Business Insider, only 11% of these CEOs have a first degree in business administration. Many people find this to be unexpected and rather amazing. When the advertisement appeared in a local paper it had a very good impact on our intended audience and many parents and students had a reinforced view that engineering is a flexible and interesting career pathway.

Credible

In order for the message to be effectively communicated and achieve its intended impact, it needs to be credible. This means that the new brain needs to believe it. If Blendtec wants to prove that their blenders are strong, running an advertisement of them blending iPhones is not only remarkably unexpected but also credible. There are a number of ways to lend credibility to a given message. In our engineering advertisement mentioned earlier, it was necessary that we referenced The Business Insider newspaper as the party that performed the research which showed that 33% of the CEOs of world's top 500 companies are engineers. This was an independent study that the public has access to and can check out for themselves. Endorsements by users or professionals can lend credibility to some products. Toothpaste companies for example, enlist the help of dentists to endorse their products.

Barry Marshal is an Australian scientist who had a revolutionary idea. While the medical community believed that stomach ulcers are caused by stress and a diet of spicy food with basically no cure, Dr Marshal had a different idea. He believed that the ulcer is caused by bacteria and are treatable by antibiotics. The prevailing wisdom was that the stomach was too acidic for any bacteria to live in it. Faced with a community that did not believe him, he did the ultimate, he infected himself with the bacteria, resulting in an ulcer in his stomach! After the disease was diagnosed, Dr Marshal treated his ulcer with antibiotics. This discovery had a huge impact on hundreds of thousands of people who have stomach ulcers and eventually earned Barry Marshal the Nobel Prize [5].

Concrete

It is easier to comprehend concrete concepts as compared abstract ones. This is particularly true when dealing with technological terminology. For example, if you are contemplating buying an iPhone, you will know that the 32GB option will have double the capacity of the 16GB. But do you really know how much is 16GB? Imagine communicating the capacity of the phone by how many photos or songs it can store or how many hours of video it can accommodate. Everyone can relate to the photos, songs, and videos because they represent concrete concepts.

Successful marketing campaigns and communication strategies need to differentiate their claims from those of the competitors in a concrete manner in order for them to be effective. So if the product or service that you are promoting is better, bigger, cheaper, faster or more effective than the competition, your message needs to deliver this in a clear and comprehensible manner. For example, if you want people to donate to charity and your message is intended to say that even a little bit can help vaccinate children in poor countries, the message can be "for the price of a cup of coffee, we can vaccinate 1 child against polio." Comparing the cost of polio vaccine to the price of something ubiquitous in our everyday life, such as coffee, makes the impact of a donation very clear and can lead to more people willing to donate. If the message is delivered through a visual medium, a picture of a cup of coffee next to a healthy vaccinated child can be very helpful as well.

Emotional

Earlier in the book we mentioned that emotions are processed in the middle brain. The relationship between emotions and decision-making was also examined. With this in mind, it is clear that messages that have a healthy dose of emotions in them will have a better chance of being remembered and changing one's behaviour. Research has shown that when we receive a message, we are most likely to remember and respond if this message was delivered emotionally. That is why organisations that are fighting a certain disease among children put pictures of children on their marketing materials when they ask you for donations.

The trick is, when you develop a communication strategy to sell a product, service or idea, you need to communicate how the audience will feel when they buy your product, use your service or adopt your idea. So if the product is a phone, do not only mention the features, instead focus also on what the user will do with the phone, this would include pictures showing the users connecting with their loved ones, reaching their destinations safely (GPS feature) and having fun with friends (entertainment apps).

Stories

We all enjoy a good story. We liked it when we were kids and we continue to like it as adults. A good story represents a better way to remember and it is always nice to share. If you are running a tutoring centre, a success story about an average student who managed to join an engineering course after taking math and physics classes at your centre is a good way to say that you provide quality service. The message can be even more credible if it is told by the student themselves.

When telling a story, or delivering a presentation, you need to pay special attention to how you start and how you end your presentation or your story. Our brains seem to pay special attention to the beginnings and ends of stories and presentations. This is probably the reason why most of the stories that our parents told us as children began with "Once upon a time...." and ended with ".......... and they live happily ever after." If you try to recall the last movie you watched, there is a good chance that you remember its beginning and end in more detail in comparison to the rest of the movie. Hollywood understands that and directors pay special attention to making the beginnings and ends of their movies more sensational.

Next time you are delivering a presentation, promoting an idea, a product or a service, you may want to begin your "show" with outlining the pain your audience is experiencing (and hopefully your product, service or idea can help alleviate it). You can use combinations of simple, unexpected, credible, concrete and/or emotional facts, data, and pictures to drive home the message. This beginning has to be short and direct so that it stays with those listening to you. The body of your presentation can discuss different features, aspects and capabilities of your idea, product or service. In concluding your presentation, you may again use a combination of simple, unexpected, credible, concrete and/or emotional messages outlining how your audience would feel after adopting your idea, product or service. This way, you will make sure that your core messages are fresh and present when your customers make their decision.

Show, not only tell

Seeing is believing and showing is a powerful tool to put the audience of a communicated message in a receptive frame of mind. Whenever possible, it is useful to get the intended users to try the product, service, or idea being promoted. Producers give free samples of their products to allow consumers to experience them. Subscription-based services such as magazines or satellite channels can give free subscription for a period of time to allow the customers to experience the service. Nowadays, most of the apps have free versions that allow the users to try the app before committing to purchase the full version. The Apple Store's Communication for Success is a very good example for this concept, where customers are encouraged to play around with the products.

Armed with the above SUCCESS framework you will be able to structure your communication strategies to achieve the desired objectives. The framework will definitely be useful if you are giving a presentation, designing a poster or billboard advertisement, directing a documentary or producing a product catalogue.

Communicate WITH A Story

Communication will stick and inspire change if it uses the

SUCCESS Framework*

 Simple

 Unexpected

 Credible

 Concrete

 Emotional

 told with a Story

 Show, not only tell

* Made to Stick by
Dan & Chip Heath

10

Shoot the Boss:
Leadership and Emotional Intelligence

"If any blame or fault attaches to the attempt it is mine alone"
General Dwight Eisenhower,
a speech to be delivered in case the Normandy invasion failed

Leaders and organisations that are aware and socially and relationally connected, are not only more liked but they are more likely to achieve their business objectives. This makes a strong business case for developing emotionally intelligent leadership. In this chapter, we will explore examples of leadership where individuals and organisations have transformed the individual and organisational narrative to achieve their goals.

Leadership and Accountability

The invasion of Normandy by the allied forces on 6th of June 1944 was a pivotal moment in the history of World War II. It opened the door to the liberation of Europe and the final defeat of Nazi Germany. General Dwight Eisenhower was the commander of the operation and while he did all that he could to plan the campaign, he had his doubts. The enemy that he was facing was well trained, well entrenched and battle toughened, the stakes could not have been higher. General Eisenhower knew that he was sending tens of thousands of allied soldiers to their deaths and their sacrifices better not be in vain. We now know the result of the Normandy invasion and the impact it had on the direction of the war. General Eisenhower gave a speech after the success of the invasion encouraging his men and acknowledging the sacrifices they made. Most interestingly though, he wrote another speech on the 5th of June, one day before sending the troops on their way. He prepared that speech to be delivered in case of failure of the invasion. The speech, which Eisenhower did not have to deliver, went like this "Our landings in the Cherbourg-Havre area have failed to gain a satisfactory foothold and I have withdrawn the troops. My decision to attack at this time and place was based upon the best information available. The troops, the air and the Navy did all that bravery and devotion to duty could do. If any blame or fault attaches to the attempt it is mine alone."

This short speech and the circumstances in which it was written are very instructive. They teach us a few lessons about what leadership is all about. General Eisenhower had doubts and the possibility of failure was real and potentially disastrous, but despite those doubts he took calculated risk and made his decision. This is leadership. He also set his mind to take the full blame for failure, should it happen. This is accountability. Leadership is the ability to provide direction and vision in the face of uncertainty. It is about making the best decisions based on the available data and sharing the credit for success with others and accepting responsibility for failure.

Shooting the Boss

The lesson we learn from the example set by Eisenhower is that accountability is a key component of leadership. While, fortunately, not all the decisions we make are of the weight of the Normandy landing, setting our internal story to accepting responsibility for failure can be a hugely empowering step, both for the leaders and for those around them.

In 2013 our school went through a major accreditation exercise. To successfully complete this exercise, academic staff needed to participate in very tedious planning and documentation processes. The time commitment to perform the preparation and documentation was not trivial and academics around the world dread it and view it as a necessary evil. We thought of a way to transform the staff experience and achieve genuine buy-in, we came up with a process that we called "Shoot the Boss!" It involved providing the staff with workshops as well as training and support sessions over 6 months to prepare them for the accreditation exercise. This included a mock accreditation exercise performed by experienced auditors. Staff were informed that the management have full confidence in them and while the success of the accreditation exercise depends on them, the management is taking full responsibility for any failure. The process concluded at a paintball court, where the entire staff force attended and each one was asked 3 questions to assess their level of preparation and readiness. I informed the members of staff that if anyone of them fails to correctly answer at least 2 out of the 3 questions, that person is required to shoot me with the paintball marker as this is a sign that I have failed to give them the proper preparation. I was the dean back then, and I wanted to show the staff that I am taking full responsibility for the accreditation exercise. Generally, the staff did very well, and one lecturer was emotional when she missed the correct answers for some questions as she thought she answered correctly and did not want to shoot me!

After the "Shoot the Boss!" session we had a couple of paintball games and went for a great lunch together. Two months later, we had the actual accreditation visit and I was really touched to receive the accreditation report. Not only was it positive with all our programmes being accredited, but with the accreditation committee recognising "highly motivated staff and students" as one of the strengths of the school. Now whenever alignment is needed, people say we need to "Shoot the Boss!". What I learnt from this session is that when the leader is willing to serve, communicates the vision clearly and shows full accountability, people are more than willing to support and pull together and even the most tedious task can become enjoyable.

Shoot the Boss!

Delivering Happiness

"You are now connected to Lili from Zappos.com." This is how my online chat session with Zappos started. I got to know about Zappos, a company that sells shoes and other clothing items from a book written by the company's CEO, Tony Hsieh. The book is titled *Delivering Happiness* and talks about how Zappos revolutionised the sales of shoes online through legendary customer service. The company achieved phenomenal growth and was later sold to Amazon for close to 1 billion US Dollars. Its extraordinary success emanated from the fact that the company used a very interesting narrative "we are not in the shoes business; we are in the business of delivering happiness." Staff are told to do whatever it takes to make the customers happy. To ensure that only those who believed in the company's mission to deliver happiness are employed, Zappos has a strange practice. One week into the four-week immersive training programme the new hires are put through, the company makes them "The Offer." If you leave now, you will be paid for the time spent plus 2,000 US Dollars! This obsession with customer service and focus on selecting staff who will do anything to deliver that is really interesting [1].

I contacted Zappos to buy a present for my son, it turned out that they do not deliver outside the United States, nonetheless my chat with Lili lasted 70 minutes. I wanted to ask her more about the company and she was happy to chat. Below are some segments from the chat that I had with Lili.

Me: I would like to by a present for my son. He is 14 years old and likes photography and soccer, what is trending that would be suitable for him?

Lili: Mushtak, we do not have any for photography but, I can recommend maybe some soccer cleats?

Me: Great!

Lili: What size does he wear?

Me: 7 or 8, depending on the design.

Lili: OK, great. Here are the options we have.

Lili: http://www.zappos.com/soccer-cleats#!/

Me: Nice!

Me: By the way, do you deliver worldwide? I am in Malaysia now.

Lili: Unfortunately, we do not currently offer international shipping. We ship to all US States and Territories. You are more than welcome to place an order using an international credit card, but the shipping address must be within the United States.

Me: :-(

Lili: I'm so sorry!

Me: I am very interested in Zappos after reading Tony Hsieh's book Delivering Happiness. Your customer service is legendary.

Lili: Thank you, we appreciate that so much!

Me: I read that your staff are offered money to quit the company in the first month, is that correct?

Lili: Yes, during the training process. If someone is willing to leave Zappos, the company will pay them. It's amazing!

Me: Amazing indeed! Were you offered that too?

Lili: Oh, yes and I didn't take it. I have been here for almost 5 years and I am very happy!

Me: What makes Zappos such a happy place to work?

Lili: I believe the independence that the company gives us. We are all treated like family.

Me: How is the value of "delivering happiness" operationalised at Zappos? With the independence you are given, how does the company ensures that happiness is delivered?

Lili: We are given the tools to make customers happy.

Me: I heard that some customers contact you guys to chat and you entertain them, is this something that the company encourages?

Lili: We do, we try to resolve the issues they might have first and then we can just chat until they are satisfied.

Me: I am going to mention my conversation with in my new book.

Lili: That's amazing, Mushtak. Please do!

Me: The idea of the book is very simple, we all tell stories in our heads that end up shaping who we are. Great leaders and great companies are able to make people change their stories to be more positive and inspirational. I believe that Zappos is a great story that all of you tell. And that is why I am very interested in the company.

Lili: Very true, everyone has their own perception of their story here at Zappos. Don't get me wrong sometimes we have issues, we have a ton of questions when things move around, but the communication is key. Everyone works as a team to get it resolved. That is the true power of Zappos.

Me: Did you change the stories that you tell yourself as a result of your work Zappos?

Lili: When I first started, yes. It was unreal how things were not the way I thought they would be.

Me: How was that?

Lili: Well, at first when you get hired they the trainers tell you that you literally can do whatever you need to make the customer happy. There was no restriction, but abuse was not acceptable. However, when I started work, I had my doubts that the company really meant that we can do anything to make the customers happy. Boy, was I wrong! That is the best part of my job, is to fix things. I had a customer tell me that I was a "YES" woman. Haha!

Me: That is really powerful. I am sure this was transformational for you.

Lili: Now, when I see new people I love to speak to them because they all have the same thought process when I was hired.

Me: You are amazing actually. What was the longest chat you had with a customer?

Lili: Thank you! It was about 5 hours, a customer needed some items for a wedding and she was about 3 months pregnant. It was really fun. She still chats in from time to time and asks about me.

Me: What else can you tell me to include in my book?

Lili: Hmm, well that we love to have fun. We have a party after the holidays to celebrate hard work. We also have a bistro and the company feeds us really yummy food. We do not have a dress code, we can wear whatever we want, style is not an issue.

Me: It is 2:49 am in Las Vegas now. Have a great morning then.

Lili: It is, very early and started my coffee.

Me: Stay awesome! I hope we can chat again in the future.

Lili: Likewise, I'm sure we will.

After finishing the chat with Lili I thought to myself, what other company encourages its representatives to chat for more than an hour without the prospect of making a sale? I will look forward to the day that Zappos delivers worldwide and I shall recommend them to anyone who wants to buy products they sell.

Competing Against Cancer

In 1990, the authors of *Tribal Leadership* were performing research for their book in which they identified four stages of organisational culture [2]. These were:

- **Stage One:** Members of a stage one organisation (tribe) are bitter, hostile and cynical. They feel detached from other tribe members and individually, they tell themselves stories of the nature "Life is unfair and I have no chance at making it any better. My work is never appreciated and life is hopeless." This is a dysfunctional stage and very few organisations can remain at this stage for long without disintegrating.

- **Stage Two:** This is where 25% of the organisations are. Members of these tribes gave up on each other. They are indifferent and have a sense of uselessness. Members blame the management all the time and while they are able to do their basic jobs, they are unable to innovate or exhibit initiative. They tell themselves stories of the sort "We are incapable of doing great work."

- **Stage Three:** This is where 49% of the workplaces are. Members of tribes at this stage are selfish and self-centred. They withhold information and knowledge from their colleagues and want to succeed without regards for the other tribe members. Individually, they tell themselves stories like "I'm great . . . and you're not."

- **Stage Four:** Tribe members at this stage share a common vision. They work together collaboratively and focus their competitive spirit against other competing tribes. They tell themselves stories like "We're great . . . and they're not."

Towards the tail end of their research process, the authors of *Tribal Leadership* interviewed the staff and management of Amgen, a pharmaceutical company, and ask them who their competitors were. If this company was to exhibit the Stage Four culture, the answer would've been "Genentech" or "Pfizer". To the authors' surprise, team after team within Amgen, when asked about who they compete against answered, "We're in competition with cancer," or "Our competitor is inflammatory disease." This led the authors to conclude that there exist a fifth tribal stage in which tribe members have a great sense of purpose that they draw the meaning of their existence from. Members tell themselves stories such as "We are here to make a difference and have a positive impact on the world and make life great for everyone."

It is very interesting to see that the level of success and impact of an organisation is reflected in and affected by the language and narrative told within these organisations. This is a further indication that changing the language used in an organisation and creating an environment within which positive narratives take root are essential ingredients of achieving sustainable success.

When a Company Abolished the P-word

Robert Newman is the CEO of MiTeGen, a small company that manufactures and distributes products for crystallisation and crystallography. He registered for the *Success with Emotional Intelligence* course and found the concept of abolishing the P-word to be "an excellent way to teach about re-framing and context, and how language matters more than we realise!" he said.

"Earlier this year we held a Kaizen Blitz event for 4 days at my company to improve many processes related to vendor management. I implemented the idea of banishing the P-word (replacing it with "Opportunity" or "Challenge") and gave each Kaizen team member $10 in ones. If someone used the word "probelm" or "can't", the one that caught the slip got $1 from them. It was a fun way to help change language and mindset. Nobody left with less than $5 as they all learned to re-frame before opening their mouths. Additionally, the practice has carried forward and my teams are getting good at re-framing and rewording without using the P-word!" Robert added.

"I did have one interesting emotional resistance to deal with though. One engineer assigned a very strong sense of personal value in the fact that he was a probelm solver and he prided himself on solving difficult technical probelms. So for that person the P-word already meant what challenge an opportunity mean to most, and "removing" the P-word felt initially like a strong personal loss. It was as if we were lowering his self-worth or value to the team by not using the P-word! In the end, and through a private discussion. I think he was able to understand how the P-word affected others negatively which was differently than how it actually inspired him.

"The manager or teacher cannot escape their responsibility of knowing each team member or student and verifying how this works, or doesn't work for the individual." Robert concluded.

11

The Awesomeness Club

"Real education is helping others rewrite their stories"

The students who took my *Success with Emotional Intelligence* course have numerous winnings to report. The course community decided to create a section on the course website that we called the "Awesomeness Club" and we agreed to report major winnings that result from the course's teachings on that section. Three years after launching the course, participants still report amazing stories on the Awesomeness Club and below are some of these stories as they are told by their heroes. I hope that these stories bring the entire human development together and show us how ordinary people managed to achieve their goals by following the simple exercises outlined herewith.

Conquering Self to Conquer a Mountain

Luis Esteban Moreno Pizarro is a 28-year-old technician from Santiago, Chile. He registered for the course to become more effective and successful but he said "I found the course to give me more than that. It gave me an important foundation for both my professional and personal life. Topics like the brain rewiring, self-awareness, social awareness, self-management and communication for success are really important for everyone." He decided to replace the p-word with the word opportunity and has been applying this technique in different area of his life, particularly mountaineering, where one would encounter many challenges, including weather, high altitude and tiredness along the journey. He now climbs with a positive attitude because he has changed his point of view from looking at things as challenges to opportunities, he says that "nowadays, climbing difficult mountains is no longer a P-word but rather a big challenge and great opportunity to develop myself... because I changed my point of view from P-word to challenge and opportunity."

One of the examples of this emotional shift was when he was climbing San Ramon Mountain which is 3,253 meters above sea level. They were 3 hours from the summit when he stopped and sat down, hungry, tired and thirsty, his friend asked him "what's up mate?" and he answered, "It's just that the summit looks too far." After walking the last day to reach the base camp, he thought it was fair to think of giving up with all the "p-words" up ahead. But he remembered the poster that he was carrying on the climb, "Don't say the P-word, just live your dreams", and at that precise moment there was an emotional shift. He found renewed strength and took that as an opportunity to challenged himself to reach the summit. He said to himself, "Hey Luis, this is a great opportunity to challenge yourself, go on and fight for it." Without that mental and emotional shift, we would not be reading his story or enjoying the wonderful picture of the San Ramon Mountain summit he has shared.

Success with Emotional Intelligence has been a great change for Luis. He went on sharing "I am more effective now and I make better decisions both in professional and personal life. Making the shift required a great will and my family has noticed the change in me, telling me that I have better disposition towards them, which is really important for me to hear."

Luis on the top of San Ramon Mountain with the message "Don't Say the P-Word- Just Live Your Dreams"

When Stammering Becomes a Friend

Michael Sony, a participant from India, found speaking in public to be a challenge due to his stammer. This is an account of how, with the help of the activities in the course, he overcame his public speaking challenge.

Michael was given an opportunity to give a speech but thought of backing off due to his stammer. However, he decided that this was the opportunity to shift his focus away from his stammer and to the positives, people were there to listen to what he has to say. So, he prepared his content and visualised himself speaking confidently to the audience, articulating each word slowly. The preparation did nothing to fend off the nerves, but he was prepared enough that when he began to speak, the fears vanished and he spoke with confidence.

Through this experience and through the course, he developed a positive attitude towards public speaking. "I see stammering now as a signal to slow down. It even can break the monotony of my speech" Michael shares.

It's been three years after Michael has completed the course, but he still keeps in touch with me. He has completed a PhD and now works as a lecturer.

Hear Only Love

Sonia is one of my many students who took the *Success with Emotional Intelligence* course. She is an only child and was very close to both her parents. Sonia says this about her mom, "My mom had grown up in a judgmental environment where she was never as good as her sister, or good enough overall. She felt the need to keep me in check. She did not want me to make 'mistakes' or choices that would make my life more challenging as I grew up."

Sonia married her husband in her late 20's but she said, "My mom was certain that he loved me but was uncertain as to whether I actually loved him." Nevertheless, they faced the same ups and downs of married life. However, her mother was quick to hold a grudge and slow to forgive during the down times, especially if what happened was due to the husband's misdoings. Sonia would try to cover up the difficulties and constantly assure her mother that everything is perfectly fine, which often came up as cheap and untrue. It came to a point where her parents' visits would cause her great mental as well as physical distress, and she would come up with work excuses to avoid being with them. Planned trips home to visit her parents would be short to avoid potential conflict. This did not fool her mother, she went on to say, "My mother brought this to my attention and mentioned that maybe I should deal with the situations or people that stressed me out or my health would continue to deteriorate. I am not certain if she realised that my interactions with her were a large part of my anxiety. She was always commenting on my weight, my hair and my relationships."

Through the course, Sonia learned the importance of developing empathy towards her mother, to see things through her perspective.

She realised that her mother was working on the limited tools she had in her emotional toolbox. "I was able to change how I perceived her actions. Her negative comments on my weight, my health, my hair was out of fear that I would be unwell or unloved. She wanted the world to see my as wonderful and amazing. She felt that she always did her best to show me that I was loved" said Sonia. It was the only way she knew how to do it but it didn't leave Sonia feeling very good. They have always had a good relationship so Sonia decided that she would not give her mother's concerns and hurtful comments power to bring her down.

On a drive with her mother to a town a couple of hours away, Sonia shared her feelings with her mother about how the constant stream of negative comments have hurt her but she also knew that it came from a place of love and fear. Her mother was not happy and asked to be let out of the car but Sonia refused, making the rest of the drive difficult. From then on, Sonia decided that whenever her mother spoke, she would repeat to herself "Hear only Love". She repeated this as often as she could throughout future conversations with her mother.

Not long after, Sonia noticed that the comments she found so negative and damaging have stopped. "I'm not sure if it is because I don't hear the negative comments anymore or that my mother doesn't say them. I think a bit of both!" Sonia concludes by saying that her relationship with her mother is stronger and she truly feels her the love and compassion her mother has for her.

The story of Sonia has generated many positive responses from the course participants but one of the more memorable ones was posted by Danielle who said, "Sonia, I am going to take a lesson from you and maybe I can have the same outcome with my father. I am far more reactive with him than with anyone else in my life. He tells me I'm too sensitive and maybe I am and I need to 'hear only love'. Thank you and I will let you know how it works."

Eating Vegetables

Another one of my online students, Andrea, confessed to having a short temper and she mentioned that ever since she started following the course, she has found herself looking for hidden opportunities in every incident that would make her angry and then smiling at the thoughts. Now and again when anger still appears, she approaches it differently. She shares an experience of her and her daughter.

She shared that her daughter is on a mission to "test her, provoke her and try her patience". One day Andrea got angry at her daughter for not doing what she had asked. She scolded her daughter but when she managed to compose herself, she explained her feelings and reactions to her daughter. Andrea said in the past she would not have been willing to listen to what her daughter had to say because of the anger, but now she is open with their communication. Andrea said that they agreed to be friends and talk things out. Half an hour after that conversation, her daughter returned to her mission to test, provoke and try Andrea's patience. "And there it was, enter anger and madness," said Andrea, "this time I didn't get to explain because she had fallen asleep, but will do it tomorrow. I was happy that I could talk to my husband about this, without still feeling angry and without snapping and yelling!" she concluded. A work in progress but a happy ending nevertheless.

Healing the Soul

Another heroine of our community is Carol Ragsdale. Carol lives in the United States and she describes herself as a 50-year-old female, a daughter, a sister, a wife, a mother and a grandmother. She goes on saying "my life is quite simple I surround myself with my family and a few chosen friends but mostly my children." She has four stepchildren, three sons and a daughter, and the biological mother of a daughter who is the oldest of the lot, and a son who is seven years younger. Carol became a single mother at the age of thirty-two after a very difficult sixteen-year marriage. She spent the next six years alone raising her children and pursuing a career as a project engineer. Later she met a wonderful man and together they shared their lives and their children, becoming quite a large family.

Carol grew up in a loving home, her father a hardworking man and a very present figure in her life, her mother a hardworking woman with a career devoted to being a wife and a mother. "I was pushed by my parents throughout my life believing that if you work hard, do as you are told and get your education, good things will always fill your life" she said. She made this the direction of her life but she would find out one night in November 2006 that there's more to learn about life than only that. Her 19-year-old son was killed in a car accident on that fateful night. She was devastated. The death of her son consumed her, the woman she was existed no more, the things that brought her joy now left a wake of pain and anguish.

Carol's journey through loss and grief was a dark, winding, lonely road. "I isolated myself from the world, from my husband, my children and my entire family. I viewed myself as a failure and blamed myself for the death of my son, after all it was my job to keep him safe from harm and I had failed to do this," she said. No one told her that there would be things in her life that she would not be able to control. She continued by saying, "I questioned every aspect of my being, including my faith. I could not understand how this could happen to me. My son was such a good boy, his life had just begun, he had made it through the tough stubborn adolescent years and was becoming such a wonderful loving, smart, generous young man. I never experienced so much darkness and pain in my life. It was at times as physically painful as it was mentally. I was stuck in a rim between life and death. I would get up after only a few hours of sleep and go to my job and perform my daily task as robotically as can be done. I would have interaction with as few people as possible and even then, I would have to fight back my tears."

Soon, her career began to show symptoms of deterioration as a result of the isolation and lack of communication with her peers, who no longer found it comfortable to have her as a part of the team. Fear and anxiety overwhelmed her and she began to wonder how she could possibly overcome another loss. Her job has been the only thing that she has managed to hold on to and it became her lifeline.

One day, while she was online searching for a way out of her pit of despair, Carol ran across the *Success for Emotional Intelligence* course. She was immediately intrigued, without hesitation or usual research, she enrolled and began taking the course. According to Carol, "I have to say nothing I had done since the death of my son had reached beyond the surface of my existence the way the first lecture on *What is Success* did." She performed the *Brain Rewiring* and *My Emotions Today* daily and felt the change flowing through her. Her family began to notice and commented on this change, but Carol still had to force herself to talk to them all. Carol acknowledges that she has still a long way to go before she reaches the end of her grief but the she says that the course has helped her to find laughter and love that she thought would never return.

Carol commented "I have learned that had I been given certain tools earlier in my life I would have been better prepared and more capable of enduring the struggles associated with my life." Now Carol plans to reach out to others to share the importance of emotional intelligence. "Our children should be taught the importance of emotional intelligence as soon as we teach them how to talk! I now believe it is even more important than the physics, science and math that we demand they learn about their emotions and how to manage themselves. At the end of the day the technical knowledge without a true-life understanding is the mechanics without any power," she concluded.

Finding Love and Getting Married

Another story that I wish to share is that of Paul Koba, a young man living in Tanzania. He was one of the first students to join the *Success with Emotional Intelligence* course. The course helped him to be aware of himself, have more self-management and social awareness, and enabled him to develop relationships with others.

Paul was in love with a young lady, but he could not confess his love to her even after three years because of fear. After watching the lecture on emotional intelligence which teaches that all emotions are okay, he finally gathered the courage profess his love for her. He bought a ring and asked her to marry him, and she said yes. She told Paul that she loved him too and that she couldn't wait to marry him and share their life together. Paul was so surprised, he had loved her for so long but he was unable to articulate it because of the fear of losing her. Paul's fiancé asked him how did he gather the courage to propose after all these years, and he told her about the course and how it teaches that all emotions are okay and that encouraged him to share his feelings.

Paul reported this on the course website right after the engagement and generously invited everyone on the course to attend the wedding in Tanzania. Paul got married in December 2013.

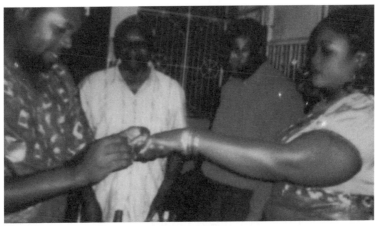

Paul's Engagement

Seeing the Light Again

Islam Ali is registered for two of my Massive Open Online Courses (MOOCs), *Success with Emotional Intelligence* and *Global Entrepreneurship*. Islam is from Jordan and she graduated with a degree in Mechatronic Engineering in 2007. I received a message from her telling me how much she enjoyed my courses and that she found them useful. I also got to know that due to the economic outlook in the region where Islam lives, and because the traditional industry is not familiar with the field of her study, Mechatronics; Islam was unable to get a job although she tried for seven years! Depression and pessimism surrounded Islam, every small issue looked like a disaster, and although she was not suicidal, she began to understand what suicidal people go through. Every birthday felt like a funeral of a wasted year as she felt that it was another year in which she did not achieve anything to be proud of.

However, after joining the MOOCs, Islam started a journey of learning and discovery with students from all over the world. She was amazed by the immediate happiness and satisfaction she felt after watching the first lecture and went on to watch 7 lectures in the first week. Being a part of a supportive learning community, she immersed herself into the assignments, group work and mental exercises. Learning about her emotions and naming them was a unique experience for Islam and *Brain Rewiring* was challenging because of her pessimism, but after a week of these activities, Islam felt a change in her perspective. She began to feel happy and hopeful all the time.

It was then that Islam decided to enrol in the *Global Entrepreneurship* MOOC. She was impressed at the fact that engineers are required to master business skills in order to support their work as engineers and she realised that being an engineer doesn't mean that she must work in the engineering industry. She decided that being a teacher with the mindset of an engineer, building generations of successful and happy people was what she wanted to do. During the duration of the MOOC, she collaborated with a student from Sudan, together, they launched a twinning program for students of the same age in Jordan and Sudan.

Realising her passion for education, she is now planning to study a higher diploma in Curriculum and Teaching Methods and attend training at Bright Innovators, a centre that teaches electrical engineering principles for children using simple ways. She plans to eventually have her own school with its own curriculum and educates using innovative teaching methods. She attributes most of the changes of her thinking to her attending the *Success with Emotional Intelligence* and *Global Entrepreneurship* MOOCs.

Achieving a Mindset Breakthrough

Shannon is another one of my online students. "There are many things in this life that I can say that I am, but confident is not one of them!" confesses Shannon. According to her, she has always struggled with sharing her emotions and allowing herself to be vulnerable. "My childhood was filled with emotional trauma. My father and brothers were ruthless and my earliest memories involved fear." She added. "My father felt that the world owed him because he had such a difficult upbringing, he would quit jobs to wallow in self-pity and guilt, he often took out his frustration and anger on me and my brothers; and my brothers, following our father's example made my life miserable as well. I was constantly belittled, ousted from family gatherings and made fun of for everything I loved, was good at or had interest in." Shannon said.

Her parents separated and her mom had custody over her and her brothers while her father moved around. As the years went by her relationship with her father deteriorated. Her brothers were always berating her, and her mother was always at work to provide for the family. When she was in grade 11, her brothers destroyed her homework assignment and her best friend had to ask the teacher to give her an extension because she was too embarrassed to go to the teacher.

This continued into her early adulthood. Shannon's father would get so angry, call her by inappropriate names and even disowned her. She was angry and decided to distance herself from him, both of them not talking for years. At 23 she was working at the local hospital working towards a career when her dad was diagnosed with lung cancer and the prognosis was that he had 3 months to live. Because of their bad relationship, she tried to make the situation between them tolerable. After he passed away she hit a pit of depression because she felt sad because "I was relieved that he had passed" she said. Guilt overwhelmed her because she couldn't find a way to make things work between them.

Shannon and her had grown close over the years, spending their free time together, reconnecting as mother and daughter. She relocated away from the family for work and things were starting to look up for her. But one morning in April 2013, she was hit with another blow, her mom had passed away. Shannon moved back to her hometown and fell into a bad depression.

Shannon started working at a Ford dealership in her hometown but was still very emotional and on anti-depressants. One day her boss sat her down to tell her that if she could not manage her emotions, they were going to let her go. This pushed her over the edge, she was so alone, angry and depressed. Shannon continued, "I tried killing myself by cutting my wrist but regretted it the moment I did it." The doctors managed to save her life and after that ordeal, she was prescribed better anti-depressants and was on the mend again. She says that until this day her brothers don't know that she tried to hurt herself. "I feared that they would belittle me and make fun of me for my weak moment. I haven't told barely anyone, I am ashamed that I was selfish enough to try to do that. I only wanted to shut the negativity off. I couldn't handle hearing one worse thing about me. The moment I did it, I truthfully thought of nothing but making the pain stop. I am very disappointed at what I did" she said.

Shannon began to heal emotionally with the help of her boyfriend, she also found a job she enjoyed and was working towards a healthier lifestyle, quitting smoking and losing 100 lbs. However, this was not the emotional breakthrough that she required. In 2016 she began to feel depressed over how her brothers and friends were treating her. She started asking herself what she could do to help her move past this state. This was when she found *Success with Emotional Intelligence* course and Shannon said from that point, great things have happened.

Shannon said *My Emotions Today* helped her to identify area that needed development and made her more aware of who she is, what she wanted and needed in life to achieve happiness. The first few days of working on her list she sought inspiration from her classmate's work and learned that there are so much more words to use than just fine, good and great. *My Emotions Today* helped but Shannon's favourite part of the course is *Brain Rewiring*. "*Brain Rewiring* was able to change my mindset. There was less doubt, drama and negativity in my life as I searched for new things that I was grateful for each day and aspired to have a fresh *Brain Rewiring* list each day," she said. "Before the course, I focused on all the challenges instead of the wonderful things in her life, after performing this exercise daily, I feel so lucky and blessed to be myself," she added.

She set out to remove these toxic relationships from her life. Shannon said that she can change all the variables in her life but she cannot change how people in her life view and treat her. For the first time in her life she wanted to argue with her inner critic, "Yes, I can do that!" "No, I'm not stupid", "Yes, these people actually like me". She said she felt this way because while sharing all of my feelings on *Brain Rewiring*, she received support and validation from the course community.

Shannon's outlook in life began to change. She has been so excited to share her dreams that she has been hiding for the fear of being ridiculed. She plans to continue brain rewiring daily and getting others to join her. She concludes by saying "Too many people say 'we can't make a difference'. But if I make 10 people smile, laugh or impact them in a positive way, and they are inspired to do the same, sooner or later that's a movement!"

Living without Regrets

Deborah Ramirez lives in Ohio. She grew up in a good family but one thing she was never exposed to is how to express her emotions. Her parents raised her and her siblings with good morals and a love for God. On the outside, they looked like the perfect family, there were no alcohol, cigarettes, or drugs in their home. Her parents were good role models with her and her siblings, they focused on how their children presented themselves but acknowledging their feelings were not encouraged and without realising it, she began to bury her feeling. She was a quiet and introverted person and that did not do anything to help her be social.

After Deborah left home and got married, she found herself modelling the lifestyle of her parents, she sent her children to church, didn't drink, smoke or do drugs. Although she lived a good life, she did not learn about the importance of emotional intelligence in everyday life.

Deborah was at work one day when her boss asked her to take an external call. It was her children's school calling to ask for her presence at the school right away. She struggled with fear and panic. When she arrived at the school, she passed her mother whose face was filled with shame, disappointment and disgust. It turns out that Deborah's oldest son had made bomb threats to his school. The first time he managed to get away with it but the second time he did it, he got caught as the school had placed a tracer on their phones after the first threat. She could not believe what was happening, she had been a good mother, raising her kids with good morals. When she got to the room where her son was, she just looked at him and said "you know better". But did he really? She went on to say, "Because I grew up hiding my emotions, my children had grown up learning to do the same."

Following this incident, Deborah's son was sent to juvenile detention and then to court. To their utter amazement, the judge turned the papers over as if the incident never happened. But the bomb threats were the beginning of her sons run in with the law. He left home at 17 and moved in with his father and has been in and out of trouble with the law ever since. Deborah is trying to live without the regrets that she could have done better as a mother. Instead of regretting her past choices, she takes every opportunity to ask others how are they feeling, whether they're happy, sad, tired, angry, etc.

Deborah's children are grown now and have children of their own. She says that this course enabled me to realise what she had missed in her childhood and with raising her own children. Deborah says, "I can't go back in time and undo all that is done, but I do not want to live with regrets either. What I learnt in this course is that I can stand here today with more gratitude than ever, cherishing the opportunity of being able to share with others my story and the personal growth I achieved through this course. Bad things do happen to good people. But with emotional intelligence and the grace of God we can slowly change our world one heart at a time!"

"I am not the same person I was when I started the *Success with Emotional Intelligence* course" says Deborah. An example she gives was that she would go out and buy boxes of wallpaper and a gallon of paint, but couldn't make up her mind because she did not have the emotional intelligence to decide what to do with it. She goes on to describe her relationship with her husband, "It was a struggle at first with my husband because I was so dependent on him. He needed me to need him. I have learned to love him in such a definite way that he is secure with me making decisions for myself. It is even okay that my decisions are not all okay, I am learning to take risk every day. I have found so much fun in making decisions that even if they weren't the best decisions that's okay!"

Today Deborah works as a life coach and works with abused women and children, helping them make better first choices. Deborah says there are no mistakes in life, only opportunities to become better. Because of this course, Deborah is pushing legislation that emotional intelligence should be taught in schools.

Giving a Hand for Life

Bashirat Abdulwahab is a participant from Abuja in Nigeria. Bashirat describes her life saying: "My entire life has been full of wars!". From losing her mother, sister and aunt one day in an automobile crash, growing up without much emotional support, to losing her husband and father.

Bashirat was working on her M.Sc thesis before the deaths of her father and brother. After their deaths, she could barely concentrate, she forgot easily and got tired quickly. She took a five month leave of absence from the course but she still tried to add something to the work on a weekly basis with much struggle. At one point the mental and physical stress was becoming unbearable, she became overwhelmed and wanted to give up on the program. But she remembered how far she had gotten, she has scored a 4.0 CGPA in her course work and giving up now would mean starting all over again.

From there she began a journey of self-discovery which included the Success with Emotional Intelligence course. *Brain rewiring* and *My Emotions Today* were tough for Bashirat in the beginning but with her diligence, soon her *My Emotions Today* report changed from relationally disappointed to relationally grateful; from physically tired to physically healthy, etc. The transformation from miserable to optimistic was real and a major shift for Bashirat.

Bashirat's life narrative began to change when she became more aware of herself. She started to be grateful for the little things; when she is mentally active, she taps into it and makes use of it for the day; when she is physically stressed or tired, she understands her body's need for a break; when she is vocationally active, she makes sure that she is impacting someone's life online or offline. She says that in this way, she has discovered that there is power in the story of her life.

Bashirat describes the most difficult part of the transition process was coming to terms with the death of her husband and her father, the very people which she leans on for support. She says "In this part of the world where I live, people expect a woman to feel and live miserable because you are a widow and I said NO to that dogma. Why should my life end because I lost hubby?". She continued by adding that people noticed her strength in these difficult times, commending her on for her faith and the willingness to succeed despite all odds.

Bashirat says that she now understands that the reason for all her traumatic experiences is to make an impact on other's, to be an inspiration to those who have suffered similar emotional trauma. She has turned her vulnerability into success and she is helping others to do the same.

The Success *with Emotional Intelligence* course has helped Bashirat discover a path to help others discover themselves. Bashirat now runs a social enterprise which helps, trains and coach women and young people. She does this through a change in mindset and emotional awareness, helping people to find a way to tap into themselves and lead better lives, especially widows and girls. She has helped these women start their own small businesses and this allows them to provide for their basic domestic needs.

Bashirat says that her traumatic experiences allow her to make an impact and to be an inspiration to people who have suffered similar trauma, especially those who are giving up on life. She goes on to say

"Well, I am a different person now because I refuse to be vulnerable. I have turned my vulnerability into success. And I am helping others to do same. And after suffering all these traumas, and making all of these impact, I should describe how I feel right now especially after recovering:

Mentally: Active

Emotionally: Inspired

Relationally: Grateful

Spiritually: Connected

Vocationally: Fulfilled

Physically: Healthy

"I connect to my emotions; my emotions complete me!" She concluded

Bashirat with the people in her community

The above stories are but samples of hundreds of great examples of members of the course community achieving success with emotional intelligence. They adopted the language of change and nudged their internal narratives to become successful, effective and happy. I am honoured by the trust they put in the course community and ever grateful for them sharing their stories with all of us. You could probably tell that I am very proud of all these course participants and I am grateful for their generous sharing. You may take a look at the course at:

https://www.openlearning.com/courses/Success

Shoot the Boss!

(This page is intentionally left blank)

Epilogue:
What Story Will You Tell?

"Those who tell the stories rule the world"

Hopi American Indian proverb

Thanks a lot for completing this book. I really do hope that you have enjoyed it. We went on a short, yet amazing, journey together where we explored how we think, feel, perceive our world and behave, and the role of the stories we tell and the language we use in all that. We also looked at the biological root for why stories are so important to our existence. I hope that by now you appreciate the importance of our stories in shaping our identities, both individually and collectively.

We explored the different levels of the human performance and development, namely, language, narratives, awareness and regulation and provided techniques to influence them positively. We ended with telling the stories of people who have managed to change their lives positively through adopting the philosophy and techniques outlined in this book.

I really hope that this book will be helpful to you as you direct your own story and help others direct their own stories. As you do that, I would love to hear from you and know about what stories are you telling. You can reach me at mushtak.alatabi@gmail.com

Dream Big. Be Different. Have Fun

Shoot the Boss!

Notes

Chapter 1: Homo Relator: What Makes Us Human

1. National Academy of Engineering, 2008. *NAE Grand Challenges for Engineering*. [Online] National Academy of Engineering. Available at: *http://www.engineeringchallenges.org*

2. Taylor, J. B., 2008. *My Stroke of Insight*. [Online] TED: Ideas Worth Spreading. Available at:

   https://www.ted.com/talks/jill_bolte_taylor_s_powerful_stroke_of_insight

3. Gazzaniga, M. S., 2016. *Tales from Both Sides of the Brain: A Life in Neuroscience*. Reprint ed. New York: Ecco.

4. Taylor, J. B., 2009. *My Stroke of Insight: A Brain Scientist's Personal Journey*. New York: Penguin Books.

Chapter 2: What Story are You Telling

1. Smith, D. L., 2011. *Less than Human: Why We Demean, Enslave and Exterminate Others*. New York: St Martin's Press.

Chapter 3: How to Program a Mind

1. Dweck, C. S., 2007. *Mindset: The New Psychology of Success*. New York: Ballantine Books.

2. Gladwell, M., 2008. *Outliers: The Story of Success*. New York: Little, Brown and Company

3. Sinek, S., 2011. *Start with Why: How Great Leaders Inspire Everyone to Take Action*. New York: Penguin Books.

Chapter 4: Success and Emotional Intelligence

1. Harari, Y. N., 2015. *Sapiens: A Brief History of Humankind.* New York: HarperCollins.

2. Goleman, D., 1995. *Emotional Intelligence.* New York: Bantam Books

3. Goleman, D., 2000. *Working with Emotional Intelligence.* New York: Bantam Books.

4. Pinker, S., 2009. *How the Mind Works.* Reissue ed. New York: W.W. Norton and Company.

5. Wagner, T., 2008. *The Global Achievement Gap: Why Even Our Best Schools Don't Teach the New Survival Skills Our Children Need--and What We Can Do About It.* New York: Basic Books.

6. Helliwell, J., Layard, R. & Sachs, J., 2016. *World Happiness Report 2016, Update (Vol 1),* New York: Sustainable Development Solutions Network.

Chapter 5: Self-Awareness

1. Flaum, J.P., 2010. *When it Comes to Leadership, Nice Guys Finish First – what predicts executive success.* [Online] Green Peak Partners. Available at: *http://greenpeakpartners.com/what-we-think/what-predicts-executive-success-green-peak-and-cornell-university-study*

Chapter 7: Self-Management

1. Mischel, W., 2015. *The Marshmallow Test: Why Self-Control is the Engine of Success.* Paperback ed. New York: Little, Brown and Company.

2. Frankl, V. E., 2006. *Man's Search for Meaning.* Boston: Beacon Press.

3. Baumeister, R. F. & Tierney, J., 2012. *Willpower: Rediscover the Greatest Human Strength.* New York: Penguin Books.

4. Ben-Shahar, T., 2007. *Happier: Learn the Secrets to Daily Joy and Lasting Fulfilment.* McGraw-Hill: New York.

5. Estrella, M., 2014. *How a Password Changed My Life.* [Online] The Huffington Post. Available at:

   http://www.huffingtonpost.com/mauricio-estrella/how-a-password-changed-my-life_b_5567161.html

6. Pink, D. H., 2011. *Drive: The Surprising Truth About What Motivates Us.* New York: Riverhead Books.

7. Louis Armstrong, *When You Smile (The Whole World Smiles with You).*

8. Ekman, P., Rosenberg, E.L., 2005. *What the Face Reveals: Basic and Applied Studies of Spontaneous Expression Using the Facial Action Coding System.* 2nd Ed. Oxford University Press: New York.

9. Lewis, M. and Bowler, P. (2009). Botulinum toxin cosmetic therapy correlates with a more positive mood. Journal of Cosmetic Dermatology, 8(1), pp.24-26.

Chapter 8: Relationship Management

1. Waldinger, R., 2015. *What Makes a Good Life? Lessons from the Longest Study on Happiness.* [Online] TED: Ideas Worth Spreading. Available at:

   https://www.ted.com/talks/robert_waldinger_what_makes_a_good_life_l essons_from_the_longest_study_on_happiness

2. Seligman, M. E., 2012. *Flourish: A Visionary New Understanding of Happiness and Well-being.* New York: Free Press.

3. Kohlrieser, G., 2006. *Hostage at the Table.* San Francisco: Jossey-Bass.

4. Brown, J. L., Roderick , T., Lantieri, L. & Aber, J. L., 2004. The Resolving Conflict Creatively Program: A School-Based Social and Emotional Learning Program. In: J. E. Zins, R. P. Weissberg, M. C. Wang & H. J. Walberg, eds. *Building Academic Success on Social and*

Emotional Learning: What Does the Research Say?. New York: Teachers College Press, pp. 151-169.

5. Warner, J., 2002. *Aspirations of Greatness: Mapping the Mid-Life Leaders Reconnection to Self and Soul*. New York: Wiley.

Chapter 9: Telling the Story

1. Anderson, C., 2016. *TED Talks: The Official Guide to Public Speaking*. London: Headline Publishing.

2. Gladwell, M., 2000. *The Tipping Point: How Little Things Can Make a Big Difference*. New York: Little, Brown and Company.

3. Heath, C. & Heath, D., 2007. *Made to Stick: Why Some Ideas Take Hold and Others Come Unstuck*. New York: Random House.

4. Gates, B., 2009. *Mosquitoes, Malaria and Education*. [Online] TED: Ideas Worth Spreading. Available at:

   https://www.ted.com/talks/bill_gates_unplugged

5. Weintraub, P., 2010. *The Dr. Who Drank Infectious Broth, Gave Himself an Ulcer, and Solved a Medical Mystery*. [Online] Discover. Available at: *http://discovermagazine.com/2010/mar/07-dr-drank-broth-gave-ulcer-solved-medical-mystery*

Chapter 10: Shoot the Boss: Leadership and Emotional Intelligence

1. Hsieh, T., 2013. *Delivering Happiness: A Path to Profits, Passions, and Purpose*. New York: Grand Central Publishing.

2. Logan, D., King, J. P. & Fischer-Wright, H., 2008. *Tribal Leadership: Leveraging Natural Groupd to Build a Thriving Community*. New York: Collins.

Image Sources

Chapter 1: Homo Relator: What Makes Us Human

A Neuron. Source: Wiki Commons, 2008. Available at: *https://commons.wikimedia.org/wiki/Neuron#/media/File:Derived_Neuron_schema_with_no_labels.svg*

Chapter 3: How to Program a Mind

A Cockroach. Source: Kane Exterminating Corp. Available at: *http://kaneexterminating.com/*

Chapter 4: Success and Emotional Intelligence

Emotional Intelligence Framework. Source: Goleman, D., 1995. *Emotional Intelligence.* New York: Bantam Books.

Chapter 9: Telling the Story

Picasso's "The Bull". Source: Bennett, J. Available at: *http://www.takeovertime.co*

Index

communist, 95

community, 24-25, 27-28, 34, 48, 69, 76, 87-89, 108, 112, 130, 145, 150, 154, 157, 162-163

company, 34, 47, 73, 87, 97, 123, 129-130, 138-144

compare, 11, 18, 29, 51, 63-64, 84, 102, 105, 112, 130-132

compassion, 3-4, 149

compel, 3, 30, 100

compete, competition, 52, 65-66, 101, 103, 130-131, 142-143

competencies, 1, 63

complex, 3, 8, 12-13, 69, 98-99, 104, 108, 118, 126

component, 9, 92, 126, 136

compose, 150

composite, 68

comprehend, 64, 107, 126, 130-131

computer, 10, 40-41, 64, 85, 97

conceive, 1, 29, 43

concentrate, 160

concept, conceptual, 1-3, 18, 23, 41, 47, 49, 62-63, 99, 126, 128, 130, 133, 144

concrete, 126, 130, 132

confabulates, 21

confess, 33, 150, 153, 155

confident, 74, 80, 137, 147, 155

conflict, 28-30, 108, 114-116, 118-119, 148

confrontation, 50, 52, 97

congruent, 22, 103

conscious, 9, 19, 53, 57, 64-65, 76

consistent, 52, 95, 124

constitution, 34

context, 4-5, 17, 31, 35, 46, 61, 80, 124, 144

continue, continuous, 1, 10-11, 16, 18, 29, 32, 40, 43, 51, 53-54, 56, 64, 74, 99, 112, 117, 123, 132, 148, 151, 156, 158, 161

control, 2, 12-13, 17, 19-20, 28, 32, 41, 53, 61, 63, 85, 91-94, 105, 151

convergence, 4

convince, 112

cooperation, 124

cooperative, 87

Cornell's School of Industrial and Labour Relations, 73

corporate, 68

corpus collasum, 17, 19-20, 23

cosmetic, 105

courage, 153

course, 1-2, 4-5, 34, 43, 46, 50-51, 57, 63, 75-76, 85-86, 94, 96-97, 109, 132, 144-145, 147-150, 152-154, 157, 159-161, 163

craft, 24, 52-53, 56, 100, 128

create, creation, 1, 10-11, 18, 23-24, 28, 30, 40, 43-44, 46, 48-51, 53-54, 64, 68-69, 75-76, 78, 87, 96, 115-117, 121, 124, 143, 145

creative, 18, 49, 52, 114

credible, 126, 129, 132

credit, 34, 93, 111, 136, 139

crimes, 28

criminal, 128

crisis, 111

criterion, 73

critic, 157

critical, 48, 65, 95

crossword, 48

cruciverbalist, 48

crystallisation, 144

crystallography, 144

cultivate, 3, 30-31, 49, 52-55, 63-64, 66, 74, 84, 92, 94, 96, 108

culture, 34, 43, 69, 80, 114, 142-143

cure, 130

curious, curiosity, 66, 76, 99, 116, 121

curriculum, 3-4, 43, 155

customer, 1, 57, 62, 84-85, 124, 133, 138-141

cystic, 103-104

Danielle, 149

deceptive, 22